THEN THE KHMER ROUGE CAME

—

Survivors' Stories from Northwest Cambodia

MARIE-MADELEINE KENNING

Matador
9 Priory Business Park,
Wistow Road, Kibworth Beauchamp,
Leicestershire. LE8 0RX
Tel: 0116 279 2299
Email: books@troubador.co.uk
Web: www.troubador.co.uk/matador
Twitter: @matadorbooks

ISBN 978 1838594 176

British Library Cataloguing in Publication Data.
A catalogue record for this book is available from the British Library.

Printed and bound by CPI Group (UK) Ltd, Croydon, CR0 4YY
Typeset in 11pt Adobe Caslon Pro by Troubador Publishing Ltd, Leicester, UK

Matador is an imprint of Troubador Publishing Ltd

To

in order of appearance

Om Borei, Ming Lin, Om Ren, Om Ri, Om Pranya,
Yiey Koum, Om Rim, Ta Jok, Om Ny and Kroo Yat

CONTENTS

—

PART ONE

2007-2014

2007-2014

EVERYONE HAS A STORY

———

Battambang, January 2008

We were surprised by his response. We were explaining how we had felt sorry for the young tuk-tuk driver taking us round Siem Reap, who had told us how the Khmer Rouge had been responsible for his parents' death and how irksome he found driving a tuk-tuk. He wanted to go and study at University but he had to support himself. Our host did not share our sentiments: tuk-tuk drivers made good money, he said, before adding: "Everyone in Cambodia has a story."

LET'S GO AND FIND OUT

——

England, December 2007

Little did we know when we left Heathrow on our first trip to Cambodia, at the end of 2007, that this journey would become an annual event. As far as I was concerned, we were on a private fact finding mission, preceded by a few days of sightseeing. We were going to take a look at the communities that our parish had recently become twinned with: Battambang, Cambodia's third largest city, and Chomnaom, a village some 60 kilometres away. No one in the parish had been there and information was hard to come by, as means of communication were rather limited in those days. We had been told that people were "very poor" and had suffered a lot. But what did very poor mean? There are poor people in England. Like doubting Thomas, I wanted to see for myself.

It would be a shame, if you have never been to Cambodia, to go to Battambang without visiting the temple complex of Angkor Wat, a UNESCO World Heritage Centre. So we flew to Siem Reap and duly purchased a three-day pass to this renowned archaeological site. The magnificence of the iconic temple of Angkor Wat, the sheer scale of the site, the wealth of sacred buildings of different periods which the pass gives you access to are truly mind blowing. Besides, spending a few days in Siem Reap before venturing further afield helps you to acclimatise and provides a gentle introduction to the kind of conditions encountered in places such as Chomnoam. We would visit Angkor Wat again, but this was not what would draw us back to Cambodia year after year.

By the time we set off for Battambang, 2007 had turned into 2008. It so happens that 2008 was also the year when we became grandparents, a development with a bearing on the writing of this book. Just as I knew very little about Cambodia, I had little idea of what being a grandmother was like. I had heard people say that it was wonderful. That you could enjoy the children and then hand them back to their parents at the end of the day. I had taken that to be more of a joke, but experience has taught me that, by the end of the day, you are indeed ready for someone else to take over. Which is, in a way, where my story begins.

BATTAMBANG

——

January 2008

The Battambang we are familiar with is not the "laid-back" town rich in colonial buildings of travel guides, but the area surrounding the offices and residence of the apostolic prefect, a priest fulfilling functions akin to those of a bishop in a missionary country. We make the odd excursion to town, a 20 minute stroll down the road or a 5 minute tuk-tuk ride for those who prefer being driven, but the compound and the district around it are where we spend most of our time. It is a poor neighbourhood, though I'm sure there are worse. Most homes, in 2008, are still made of wood. Some are on stilts, with a sheltered area downstairs for preparing food and relaxing, while others consist of just one ground-floor room. The furniture is basic: a bed, a few boxes or cupboards, sometimes a few plastic chairs. The houses are packed close together: people live cheek by jowl here. In the rainy season the narrow dirt tracks between the houses become full of puddles that, at times, force you to cut through someone's open area. People don't seem to mind. As we walk around, we are occasionally assailed by the smell of urine,

probably from some nearby toilets. Not much more than holes in the ground, one suspects.

Most people travel to Battambang by coach, minibus, or taxi. As you reach the city, coming from Phnom Penh along National Highway 5, you pass a roundabout with the gigantic statue of a man kneeling on a round platform. You will almost certainly notice that he has a cup in his hands with a stick across it, in keeping with his name: Lokta Damborng Krornhung, 'Grandfather stick'.

According to a local legend, Lokta Damborng, a poor cowherd, was looking after his herd when he picked up a stick with magical powers enabling him to control how the cattle moved. After a while, he became ambitious and used the stick to usurp the throne. Unfortunately for him, the magical stick lost its magical qualities when the legitimate king returned home a few years later. Forced to flee, the power-hungry cowherd threw away his stick, which floated down the river to where

Battambang city is located. Hence the name Battambang, which is pronounced "Batdamborng" and means 'the lost stick'.

Our very first trip to Battambang was not along National Highway 5, but along the Sangkae river, which passes through Battambang on its way to the Tonle Sap, the huge freshwater lake near Siem Reap. Our first memory of the city, therefore, is not the iconic roundabout, but a steep embankment with a few people waiting at the top. No obvious sign that we had reached our destination, no jetty, no announcement. Just some steps.

We had decided to travel from Siem Reap to Battambang by boat rather than by road, lured by the appeal of a trip described by guidebooks as very picturesque and taking around four hours. Not including, of course, the usual minibus pickup tour of umpteen hotels on the way to the port at the crack of dawn. Picturesque it certainly was, although not quite the kind of picturesque we had anticipated. More the noisy and uncomfortable type of picturesque. As for the four-hour

8

duration... We had been warned it might last up to seven hours, but even that turned out to be an underestimate. To be fair to the guidebooks, we had got glimpses of life on the river. We had sailed along narrow waterways with branches that lashed against the sides, causing those sitting at the end of rows to duck to avoid being hit on the head. We had passed various kinds of fishing boats, fishing nets, floating villages, even a floating church. Still, to refer to the boat journey between Siem Reap and Battambang as a "scenically stunning way to avoid the bumpy roads" is, to my mind, a wee bit over the top. *Memorable* would be more appropriate.

You are probably imagining that we travelled on a nice, shining white vessel of the kind commonly used in Europe on river cruises. I know I did. After all, this was the type of boat shown on our ticket. Hence my anxiety when, on reaching the port, our luggage was loaded on board a small wooden craft, with

some primitive form of protection from the sun and the wind. Not a life jacket in sight, but, on the plus side, a small cabin with a hole in the floor for not so comfortable "comfort breaks".

"Is this it?" said my husband. Perhaps they had made a mistake and our belongings were being put on the wrong boat. Siem Reap port at that time was not the sleek development it has become. Just a row of huts and shacks with a few boats drawn up on the shore. No visible evidence of organisation for the untrained eye, no officialdom, and no booth collecting an embarkation fee. It is a very different kind of place nowadays, and I have wondered what happened to the people who lived along the waterfront. Where have they gone? Were they just moved on to make room for the modern world? I doubt they fared better than the people living in floating villages on the lake, who used the landing place for free for years, but, on our last visit, were now charged a fee, even when going to hospital, without deriving any benefit from the new facilities, where their small craft would have to wait until all the tourist boats had been attended to.

As you probably guessed, it wasn't the wrong boat, picture or no picture. And instead of taking four hours, the journey lasted around nine. It was the dry season and water levels were low. Not that this was a problem on the Tonle Sap, which stretches almost to Phnom Penh, with a surface area and dimensions that vary with the season. If anything, there was rather too much water for our liking, as we pondered our chances of successfully swimming to the distant shore gliding past on our right hand side, should the boat spring a leak or capsize. It was one of those moments when you think: "What on earth are we doing here, are we completely mad?"

The fear that we might drown disappeared after entering the Sangkae river, to be replaced by concern over the ability of the crew of two to fix the engine when the boat got stuck in weeds and it overheated and died. Once, and then again, and then a third time. It took a while, but each time the engine was eventually coaxed back to life.

With a four-hour trip in mind we had packed enough food for, well, obviously … a four-hour trip. In other words, virtually nothing. This being our first time in Cambodia, we took health risks pretty seriously – that is except for accepting to embark on a boat completely devoid of any safety equipment. We had encountered food poisoning during a holiday in India a few years before and had no desire to repeat the experience. So we stayed well clear of any local food when the boat stopped at a floating restaurant, encouraged in our resolve to confine ourselves to crisps by the discovery that the toilets were – no big surprise here – a hole in a cabin round the back. We were fully aware of what happens to sewage near bodies of water. Nevertheless, finding ourselves face to face, so to speak, with reality, was a strong incentive not to sample the food on offer.

Knowing hunger and malnutrition to be widespread in Cambodia, I am reluctant to talk of having arrived hungry at our destination. True, we hadn't eaten a proper meal for over ten hours. But we had had three meals the day before, and were about to be fed by our host. Our need for food was temporary and of no consequence, unlike that of many Cambodians. It was also the result of a personal decision: after all, we could have chosen to eat in the floating restaurant. Indeed, it could be argued that we should have, since the people working there depended on the dishes they sold for their livelihood.

Trips to Cambodia present you with many such dilemmas, to be wrestled with not only as you face them, but also after you get back home. For such incidents stay with you, hovering at the back of your mind, ready to surface given the right prompt. I remember, for instance, staring at my food at breakfast one morning during one of our early trips, unable to bring myself to eat more of it. I had ill-advisedly ordered some kind of chicken soup or pork soup as a change from my usual omelette. When I started to eat the soup, I found the contents to include cuts of meat you just would not serve in Europe. I am not a particularly fussy eater, but this was way beyond my comfort zone. In poor countries, nothing is wasted, and it is not uncommon to discover lumps of fat, chicken feet, etc. in the dishes supplied by humble establishments. I eventually gave up on my soup, guiltily aware that the people I had seen recently in the local hospital would jump at the chance of eating it. They only received one meal per day and had to rely on their family or on charitable donations for anything more.

The hospital trip was still in the future when the pick-up truck which had come to fetch us drove into the Battambang church compound, but the baptism of fire we were about to receive would give us a taste of things to come. We had hardly sat down to eat after our unintentional fast, when a group of ladies appeared at the door, with the news that the wife of a handicapped man living nearby had just died. "What did she die of?" I would ask, when we accompanied our host, Fr Totet, on a visit to the bereaved husband the next day. They didn't know. She had just got sick. She was thirty-five.

The meal over, we were led to a nearby building to watch a dance display by young landmine victims. Full of graceful hand movements, the show combined two keys aspects of the work of the prefecture: the promotion of traditional Cambodian culture and the integration of people with disabilities. The display was a model of collaborative effort, with those who could walk guiding the wheelchairs of those who could not, and the dancers without hands stamping their feet instead of clapping. I can still picture a dance involving two youths, a girl and a boy, skipping in and out between two long poles held by two other youngsters who knelt on the floor and banged the poles down, clacking them in and out rhythmically. The female dancer had a prosthetic leg; her partner's arms had been amputated below the elbow, and I recall becoming absurdly concerned that he might lose his balance and have nothing to break his fall.

Afterwards, the participants would tell us that they had inadvertently stepped on a landmine while gathering firewood, or had found a grenade and, not realising what it was, had hurled it against a tree. For the moment, their attention was focussed on the choreography, on making the correct gestures. They had rehearsed for the occasion, and you could tell how they relished the opportunity to perform in front of an audience. Their life stories were sad, but their dancing was joyous, an unmistakable affirmation of life.

Over the following days, we attended a wedding, went round a range of educational establishments, and had a look at some projects. We also went to Mass. Among the congregation was a small group of women of my age who seemed to gravitate towards me at the end. They were delighted to discover that I was born and brought up in France. "Oh, française!" they exclaimed, before talking to me in French. Considering that they had not spoken the language for some fifty years, their fluency was remarkable. And as people of their generation rarely speak English, and our Khmer was then virtually non-existent, it was a godsend for communication.

When I enquired how they came to know French, the language of the former colonial power, they explained they had learnt it at school with the Sisters of Providence. The Sisters of Providence (*Soeurs de la Providence de Portieux*) are a congregation founded in France in 1762. Dedicated to the teaching of poor children and health care, the Congregation ran schools, orphanages and hospitals throughout Indochina. It opened a school in Battambang in 1905, when the country was a French protectorate, and the number of Sisters working in Cambodia before the Khmer Rouge takeover is said to have been over one hundred. One of the nuns who had taught the parishioners gathering round me was still alive at the time of our visit. Small and slender, with a smiling, slightly inscrutable countenance, she was now eighty years old and reminded me of one of my aunts. I was struck by the way she radiated calm, peace, openness to whatever might lay ahead. She told me her life story, which had been less than straightforward and peaceful, pausing from time to time to check that I had understood, and to apologize for the inadequacy of her more than adequate French. I often wish I had her calm.

One of my most vivid memories of that period is sitting down on the floor in someone's home with a few of the French speaking ladies, singing children songs such as *Frère Jacques*. Their excitement as they sang and clapped their hands was childlike and amazing. At the time I put it down to their not having had an occasion to do this for a long time, and to the usual pleasure that older people take in reminiscing. I have thought about this again since the interviews, and have come to the conclusion that there was rather more to it.

THE WIDOW

——

Chomnaom, 2009

It was during one of our first trips to Cambodia, the second year I think. We had come on a day visit to Chomnaom. The first part of the journey had been fine: the road was tarmacked and reasonably smooth, and we were sitting in the cabin of an air-conditioned truck, not in the open air at the back, exposed to the elements and the pollution around.

Turning off the main road brought a dramatic drop in comfort level. No more tarmac but a dirt road with potholes galore that would not be upgraded until 2015. Our vehicle, like all the others, inevitably sent dust flying around, dust that enveloped any cyclist in the vicinity – and there were quite a few – and settled on the vegetation and the homes lining the road. As in Battambang, the majority of the dwellings were made of wood. Some were again single-storey huts. Others stood on pillars, with a raised section for sleeping and an open area underneath for cooking, eating and socialising, a common configuration well suited to the climate. In the better houses the open area had wooden platforms, chairs, or concrete benches.

16

You could sit there in more comfort than on the ground, especially in the rainy season. Or else you could lie down in one of the hammocks stretched between the pillars and enjoy a pleasant rest in the breeze and the shade. Unless, that is, your house happened to be situated near a busy dusty road.

Approaching Chomnaom left you in no doubt about the poverty of the place. At that time, Chomnaom did not have electricity. Power lines only made an appearance in 2012, although the high connection costs, not to mention the price of electricity itself, supplied from nearby Thailand, initially prevented a number of families from embracing this "modern" development. In the local primary school only the staff room was wired at first. When we expressed surprise at this, we were told that the school budget (reportedly two dollars per child per year at the time) would not have allowed the school to use electricity in the classrooms.

No electricity means, of course, none of the appliances that the rich world takes for granted: no cooker, no fridge, no washing machine, no dishwasher. Not that the last two would be much use, even now, as to this day Chomnaom does not have running water. People collect rainwater from the roof during the rainy

season and store this in huge stone jars on the ground around the house. But this does not see them through the year. The lucky ones will have a pond and a pump to turn to. The others have little choice but to walk down to the river with pails, or, if they live near enough, lay a hosepipe on the bank. Whatever its source, water for cooking and drinking has to be boiled. Clean bottled water is available, but too expensive. Furthermore, in the absence of rubbish collections, throwaway non degradable plastic bottles end up as unsightly piles of litter.

As we go round the village we are puzzled to discover that virtually all the houses, even the most dilapidated ones, sport a television aerial. "TVs? Without electricity?" Until someone explains that the possibility of running TVs off 12 volt car batteries has prompted enterprising individuals to set up businesses which, for a relatively modest sum, come and collect flat batteries to recharge them from a generator. Looking at the TV screens along the road, I see what are clearly foreign programs, showing environments and lifestyles totally unlike what surrounds us. I can't help but wonder what impact all this is having on people. What do they make of what they see? How does it make them feel?

We move on to a tour of the grounds of the Catholic church, a compound approximately 100 metres long by 80 metres wide, enclosed within a low stone wall with railings on top. The place has a very open feel due to the presence of few buildings and their small size. Around the compound are magnificent tall palm trees, so typical of the Cambodian landscape, that make the countryside look like paradise. It is not so paradisiac, of course, when you are out in the midday heat. Even during the dry, cooler season – which is when we come – the temperature is often in the mid 20s in the shade and you certainly feel it. How could you not, with sweat trickling down your back?

The two main buildings of the compound are a simple, beautiful, wooden church on a raised concrete platform half way down the right-hand side, and, on the left, a two-storey building made of stone and wood. This is the so-called administrative block and comprises a dozen or so multifunction rooms which serve as classrooms, offices, dining room and sleeping quarters, their use changing, after some shifting of the furniture, with the needs of the moment.

As we move around, our guide, Fr Pedro, a Colombian missionary, points out some crumbling structures housing the kitchens, stores, toilets, which have top priority in his upgrading wish list. I notice a couple of young children, a girl who might be five or six years old and a boy who looks about four. Rather unkempt, they have clearly been left to their own devices and have attached themselves to us. The little boy becomes quite talkative when we approach the toilet block, eager to pass on what he clearly regards as important information. I guess he is explaining what toilets are for. I ask who the children are. They are the grandchildren of a widow living in a small house behind the church. As she does not have any income, the Church employs her to sweep the yard and gives her bags of rice in exchange. It does not seem an awfully generous deal, but there are many others like her to support, as well as 80 kindergarten children, some Catholic, most of them Buddhist, to look after and feed. All this when the income from the collection taken during Mass does not even cover the cost of the fuel used to get here.

We pass the lady's house as we tour the village in the evening. She is sitting on the ground in front of her house, with three young children. It is getting dark, dinner time. There is a bowl in front of each family member unlikely to contain more than rice. Later we will learn that the widow's daughter left for Thailand a couple of years ago. The daughter did come back once, 12 months or so later, but hasn't been heard from since.

We do not take pictures of this humble and humbling scene. It would be inappropriate, somehow, voyeuristic. As for the lady's story, it will turn out to be more and more common as time goes on. Thailand, where wages are substantially higher than in Cambodia, is not far away, and working there, legally or illegally, seems an enticing prospect when you have virtually nothing, and very little hope of work locally. Thailand's beckoning power, which grows with every failed rice crop – a frequent setback as a good harvest depends on rain coming at the right time – is enhanced by the relative affluence of those who return, and perhaps also, who knows, by what people see on TV.

This prompts more people to try their luck. Those working abroad normally begin by sending money home, or come back flushed with funds. But not all of them carry on making payments to the family they have left behind, especially if they enter into a new relationship. When both parents go away, children are usually left behind with relatives. Who would look after them in Thailand while their parents are at work? Where would school age children go to school?

And so an increasing proportion of the older generation find themselves having to take care of grandchildren. Not for a few hours, but 24/7.

A WHOLE NEW BALL GAME

Cambodia and England, 2015-2017

It was to document the everyday difficulties of these grandparents – more often than not, grandmothers – that I started interviewing, with their consent, some of the 50, 60 or 70 year olds we were acquainted with. By 2015, I had eight grandchildren of my own, ranging in age from a few months to a six-year-old and I looked after them from time to time. Not all together, at least not by myself; just one or two, three at the most. This often left me wondering how on earth I had managed to bring up four children. I had forgotten how exhausting it is to take care of young kids, how it does not leave you any time for yourself when they are no longer babies and do not sleep as much. Not to mention having to lift them up and carry them, or the occasions when they are out of sorts or simply play you up. "When do I put him down? When is his bedtime?" I asked one of my daughters the first time I babysat for her new baby, while she went out with her husband for the evening. "Oh 8 o'clock", she said. Except that Baby had other ideas. 8 o'clock came and went; so did 8.30, 9 and 9.30. All attempts to put him in his cot only provoked persistent crying, which I found myself unable to ignore, though if it had been my own child, I might have well have closed the door eventually and left him to it. At least for a while. When our daughter came back at 10 o'clock, my husband and I were still taking turns pacing up and down the kitchen with Baby in our arms.

These moments convince you that there is indeed a time for everything, and that the time for bringing up children is not 60+. So when I met Cambodian grandparents left in charge of a young brood, I naturally wondered how they coped. All the more so as I knew that, even without the demands associated with bringing up young children, these people had a tough life: barely enough to eat, water shortages during the dry season, floods during the rainy season, unsafe water, lack of domestic appliances, inadequate sanitation. As well as insufficient healthcare, minimal state-run social services, and no state or private pension providing them with any kind of secure income.

As it turned out, the difficulties of looking after children at that point in life were to become a minor theme in our conversations. It was a burden that they took in their stride after all they had endured. It almost paled into insignificance compared to what they had lived through. This was what needed to be known, shared, acknowledged. Heart-rending accounts, hard to listen to, that revived painful memories. I would ask: "Are you sure you want to continue?" They were.

I doubt I would have entertained the idea of interviewing Cambodian grandparents, had I not had experience of conducting interviews in my professional life. I knew how to go about it, or so I thought. I was aware of the need to inform prospective interviewees of the purpose of the interviews and how they would be used, to stress that participation was entirely voluntary, to explain, in my case, that the subjects would not be paid but that profits, if any, would go to supporting the poor in Cambodia, and, of course, to obtain their consent.

I knew it was best to start the actual interviews with a few basic questions to help people settle down. Consequently, we began with innocuous items like their name, their date and place of birth, their parents' occupations. The conditions were as good as could be expected: the setting was a familiar one, we were known to most of the interviewees, the atmosphere was relaxed. What I had overlooked, however, is that providing information about when and where you were born, for instance, is only straightforward if you can read and write, are used to providing identity details, are able to give clear succinct answers and, if necessary, to expand on your answers and clarify them. It is not quite so simple otherwise. This was a very different context from my home ground and it soon became obvious that it wasn't all going to be plain sailing.

Even names proved to be a problem. And I am not talking here about writing down strange sounding names correctly. I mean establishing a person's full name, although in the end we decided that there was no need for this to be recorded. We moved on to their date of birth, which they seemed to regard as an odd question, and which it took them a while to work out. Sometimes fairly haphazardly, for the outcome of their pondering did not always tally with what they said their age was, or with the age they subsequently stated as the age they had got married. Or some other event involving a date. It was an issue we would revisit on a number of occasions to try and eliminate inconsistencies. They fared better with place of birth, which they stated without hesitation and quite precisely. Too precisely, in fact. We did not know where the place was and, more problematically, neither did the interpreter. They were taken aback by our ignorance. It was common knowledge. I'm sure it was. Among the locals.

As we were to discover, there were good reasons for all these difficulties. Unfortunately, they added to the length and complexity of the interviews to an extent I had not anticipated.

The initial questions over, we were to move swiftly to the present, and the problems of raising children in your third age. The interviews were not intended to encompass their whole life. I was interested in the here and now. But in-between their early life and the present time lay a critical period, tragic events waiting to be told, clamouring for attention. I would not have dared to ask them about the Khmer Rouge Revolution, judging it too sensitive a subject. They did not have my qualms. It had coincided with their youth or early adulthood, and they did not want what had gone on swept under the carpet.

I was concerned that revisiting this dark period might cause them to be re-traumatized but they were adamant. You could tell by the way they maintained eye contact with me that they wanted me to understand what it had been like, while their tone of voice, their occasional vehemence, their gestures and facial expressions showed how vividly present the past remained.

They digressed, they branched out. I tended to let them speak, unless they had clearly lost the thread, or had become impossible to follow. Not just because it would have been rude to interrupt, but because these dreadful memories were one of the facets of the legacy left by the Khmer Rouge.

Cross cultural communication is known to be fraught with difficulties and this was no exception. How could it not be when our cultural backgrounds were so dissimilar? Misunderstandings occurred, which would have to be cleared up when they came to light; incorrect assumptions were made as to what the other party did or didn't know. Factor in the need to translate what was said into Khmer or into English, and the use of informants eager to tell their story who had no experience of working with an interpreter and no awareness of the limits of short-term memory. They would launch into their replies, engrossed in what they were saying. Gently and very politely the interpreter would intervene, explain his predicament, and invite them to go back to the beginning and break what they had to say into manageable chunks. They agreed, but, more often than not, would forget to pause once they were in full flow. Lastly, sprinkle in the odd additional question from me, a risky move liable to send them on new labyrinthine trails, and you will get a sense of what it was like.

We carried on with twists and turns and all manner of meanderings. But then, how many people would be able to explore the deepest recesses of their memory with its mazes of intersecting paths and shape the results into neat rectilinear accounts? I am not sure I would, although I did not appreciate this at the time.

What follows is a small set of life stories shared with me for wider dissemination that offer insights into my interviewees' mental worlds rather than exact descriptions of what happened to them. Recollections filtered through time and inevitably subject to the limitations of memory. Translated, jotted down, reconstructed, and interwoven with some personal memories. For gradually their stories became part of my own story.

PART TWO

2015

OM BOREI

———

Battambang, January 2015

We began with interviewees living in Battambang as this is where we spend most of our time. Being on the spot made it easier to contact people and to make a start while working out our Chomnaom schedule. The interviews in this first round all followed the same pattern. Where we met, however, was left up to the interviewees: some chose to be interviewed at home, others opted to meet in the presbytery or in some other suitably quiet environment. As our knowledge of Khmer does not extend much beyond everyday niceties of the "How are you?", "Do you have children?" type, we communicated through a bilingual student with experience of acting as interpreter. I was responsible for planning and conducting the interviews, confining myself to jotting down the odd point, while Michael, my husband, took comprehensive notes and a few photos.

We started with an old acquaintance of ours, relatively speaking, called Om Borei. We met this friendly lady on our very first visit to Battambang. Noticeably shorter than the average in a country whose population ranks among the shortest in the world, Om Borei has black hair, like most of her compatriots, and when she smiles, which she frequently does, you can see that several of her teeth are missing or sport gold fillings. An incomplete set of teeth is quite common here among the older generations, who never had the opportunity to have their teeth looked after. Even now, dental services in Cambodia remain so woefully inadequate that foreign dentists bringing over their own instruments to offer free treatment to the poor have said to us that they find themselves frustratingly restricted to doing mainly extractions.

Along with many women her age, Om Borei typically wears a multi-coloured blouse with either a long skirt, often with a different pattern, or some loose fitting trousers. She dresses more formally on Sunday, at least for Mass, when she wears a white blouse and a plain straight skirt. Unlike her clothes, her footwear stays the same: a pair of sandals, always left outside, as is customary, before entering a house or a church.

Om Borei will for ever be associated in my mind with the voluntary work she does at the hospital. Not long after meeting her, we were told how, every morning, she went over to the presbytery to collect some money to distribute to destitute hospital patients who, otherwise, would only get one meal a day. She also collected second hand clothes, which she washed before handing them out to those most in need.

We accompanied her to the hospital once, a trip that stands out for me as one of my most depressing experiences ever. Michael has gone back there since and tells me the situation has improved a little, but this particular visit was grim beyond belief. The outside environment wasn't bad. It was, in fact, comparatively pleasant, the facilities being housed in a set of low white buildings surrounded by green space. Inside, the corridors had been swept, but the sweepings had been left in a corner. On each side of the corridor a series of small rooms full of people, not patients, for the most part, but family members who had come to attend to the needs of loved ones, to feed, comfort, and generally take care of them. Simple beds – but then beds tend to be pretty basic in rural Cambodia, often just a mat rolled out every night – virtually no equipment of the type you associate with hospitals, patients moaning in pain, and not a single nurse or doctor in sight. The only white coat we came across was standing outside one of the buildings trying to get the body of a patient who had recently died moved to the crematorium. The family had no money to pay for the transport and were at a loss as to what to do, and the white coat was getting very frustrated. When the Jesuit brother who had brought us to the hospital found out what was happening, he offered to transport the corpse in the back of his truck and pay for the incineration and the attendant costs. What would have happened if he hadn't, I have no idea.

The visit left me with a feeling of total helplessness, so great were the patients' needs, but also with admiration for our guide. The way in which patients greeted Om Borei as she went around, saying hello to one, enquiring how another was doing, listening to someone else telling her how they needed an operation which they could not afford, giving small amounts of money here and there, left you in no doubt as to the value of what she was doing. And the fact that she was doing it willingly, when all I wanted to do was get away, made it all the more impressive.

We had agreed to interview Om Borei at home. The house was easy to find, we settled down and got going. We had barely started, however, when Magkara, Om Borei's daughter, walked in. Unlike her mother, Magkara is fluent in English and after listening to a few exchanges, she began to chip in from time to time. This unforeseen development, no doubt partly due to the setting, presented me with a conundrum. Should I just accept the situation? Or should I ask Magkara to leave the room in order to preserve the integrity of the methodology? I was not conducting a conventional research study and the last thing I wanted to do was to cause offence by making an inappropriate request that might ruin the whole enterprise. I decided to say nothing and just monitor Magkara's interventions.

Over the course of the project, there would be other times when an interview would be attended by unexpected guests and turn into a family affair, with relatives, friends even, taking an interest in what was going on, and, on occasion, putting in their two cents. I am sure that Magkara did not come to sit with us because she did not trust the interpreter. I think that she partly acted out of curiosity – like most of us, she did not want to be left out of what might be an interesting conversation – but that she was also motivated by her desire to provide filial support. She had heard her mother's recollections before and wanted to make sure that Om Borei did herself justice. I can't deny that Magkara's presence had an impact on the interview. Among other things, it influenced the amount of detail proffered. But whenever Magkara jumped in to reply to the question I had asked, or to expand on what her mother was saying, I made a point of checking with the latter, getting her to confirm or rephrase what had been said.

Like the rest of her generation, Om Borei, who was born in 1953, has lived through some of the darkest years in Cambodia's history. But her hardships did not start with the Khmer Rouge. Having lost her father at the age of three, she was brought up by a mentally disturbed mother until, in her early teens, she moved in with a local Catholic family to look after the children. The arrangement lasted for about two years, at the end of which Om Borei was taken in by the Sisters of Providence, who in those days ran an orphanage. After a spell in the kitchen, she became involved in caring for the 5 to 11 years old, including teaching them catechism as well as what our interpreter translates as literature, but which, I suspect, was probably literacy.

At this point, Om Borei suddenly becomes emotional. She does not explain why, but she has said that the Sisters took pity on her and I assume that she feels grateful to them for the way they stepped in when they saw she needed help. Besides looking after orphans, the Sisters ran a hospital in the church compound. Om Borei started working there from 1970, at first doing the cleaning, and then graduating to performing duties such as giving injections. Her nursing experience would prove crucially important later on, and may even have saved her life, although, obviously, she had no inkling of this at the time. But she must have done well for, in 1973, she officially joined the nursing staff.

Here Om Borei's story becomes quite involved, a fitting reflection, I guess, of the confusion and unrest that were affecting the area and of the changes in fortune of the various forces. She mentions treating patients injured in the war and we are unclear, at first, which war she is talking about. Like most people, we have heard of the atrocities committed by the Khmer Rouge, Cambodia's ruling party between 1975 and 1979. But she is talking of a time before the notorious Khmer Rouge era. It turns out that what she is referring to are the years of insurgency under the Lon Nol government that preceded the Khmer Rouge takeover.

The innumerable instances of human rights abuse that took place under the Khmer Rouge have rightly drawn attention to its four-year reign. Sadly, however, unrest, fighting and the trail of suffering left in their wake were not confined to the years when Pol Pot ruled Cambodia. They started long before, just as the overthrow of Pol Pot did not suddenly usher in peace.

The fact is that the Khmer Rouge gained power within the context of a long period of struggle for independence, a struggle that encompassed much of South East Asia, with North Vietnam at its epicentre. Although Cambodia achieved independence

33

fairly smoothly in 1953 thanks to the political acumen of its Head of State, King Norodom Sihanouk, it then found itself drawn into the protracted wars that engulfed Vietnam, where the conflict with France (1946-1954) was replaced by a bloody, divisive war against US troops (the Vietnam War) that would only end in 1975 with the fall of Saigon (now Ho Chi Minh) and the reunification of North and South Vietnam.

Officially neutral, Cambodia was in fact covertly used as a base with the tacit permission of Norodom Sihanouk by both the (North) Vietnam People's Army and the Viet Cong (South Vietnam National Liberation Front). In 1970, a pro-Western, anti-Vietnamese military coup led by General Lon Nol removed Sihanouk as Head of State and brought Cambodia's neutrality to an end. Supported by the US and by South Vietnamese forces, the Khmer Republic set out to defeat the communists, dragging the country into civil war. Five years on, the Republic would be overthrown by the Khmer Rouge, which would be ousted in its turn in 1979, when Vietnamese forces invaded the country. However, conflict and atrocities were to continue, notably in the North West of Battambang province, the region we visit, where the Khmer Rouge factions are said not to have laid down their weapons until 1998. We are talking, therefore, of a period well within living memory and many people still bear the scars.

Om Borei's fate when the Khmer Rouge forces arrived has a familiar ring if you have read books on that period: expulsion to the countryside, separation from other family members – in her case, her mother – hard manual work that included carrying water from a water source 3 kilometres away, digging, planting rice and building roads. All this with little to eat, especially as she tried to save rice to take to her mother. As her account returns time and time again to her mother's poor state of health, I wonder whether her concern over her mother together with her ability to offer her help from time to time was one of the

things that got Om Borei through. She was also sustained by her
faith. Having been brought up among Catholics, it was natural
for her to turn to God at a time of trouble. She tells us how she
prayed and prayed, albeit secretly as religion was banned. Her
nursing career stood her in good stead, enabling her to be of
service to those around her, including attending to some of the
soldiers. This did not stop her being interrogated and harassed
after being accused of being a prostitute, perhaps even a madam.
"How come?" I ask, when I see her again the following year.
"Oh", she says, "the team leader asked me whether I had ever
had a boyfriend and did not believe me when I said I hadn't." So,
inadvisably, Om Borei changed her answer from no boyfriend to
15. She now laughs about it, but joking with the Khmer Rouge
was not a good idea, and it cost her three days of detention and
questioning before being sent back with a warning that she had
been lucky: she had narrowly escaped death. The outcome may
have been different, perhaps, had she not been able to care for
the sick and been more useful alive than dead.

Om Borei eventually returned home when the Vietnamese
liberated Battambang in 1979. In Battambang she met again
a former patient of hers, they fell in love and married. Sadly,
this wasn't nearly the end of her troubles. Two years later, her
husband, a sailor by trade who plied routes between Cambodia
and Thailand, was stopped from getting back into the country,
possibly, though she does not actually say so, because of doubts
about his allegiances. Maybe he wasn't stopped but simply seized
an opportunity to leave Cambodia, to flee, hoping she would find
a way to follow him. Who knows? There are so many unknowns
in all the stories, so much left unsaid, unexplained. Whatever
the case, he sent word of his whereabouts to his relatives, but the
relatives kept the letter and did not tell Om Borei. This too is hard
to understand, which does not make it untrue. By the time the
letter was passed on to Om Borei, it had become illegible. There

was to be a further, unexpected, development: in 1987, some six years after his disappearance, Om Borei's husband made a second attempt to contact her, enquiring through a friend whether she had married again and inviting her to join him in Thailand. She had not remarried, she had remained single. They had a child, a daughter, born after he went missing, whom she was bringing up on her own. She could have accepted the offer. However, she had an epileptic mother who needed looking after and filial ties are strong here. She did not go.

She had taken up buying and selling foodstuffs, a common occupation for women, both then and now. As money had been abolished, all trading, at first, involved bartering one type of goods for another. Om Borei's first foray into business involved exchanging fish for rice. Every day, she would walk 6 kilometres with 25 kilograms of rice on her back, swap the rice for fish, and then take the fish 7 kilometres to the market. She now suffers from back problems, which she puts down to the heavy loads she has had to carry. It seems to me possible that over time her spine has become compacted from all this carrying, thereby affecting her stature, but this is only speculation on my part as she herself makes no reference to any adverse impact on her height.

Remarkably, Om Borei did more walking on Sunday in order to attend Mass 13 kilometres away. After a year, she switched from selling fish and rice to selling cakes, and then duck eggs. She was careful with the proceeds of the sales, saving most of what she earned. By getting the duck eggs on credit and borrowing some money from relatives, she was able to start building her own house. "A very small house", she specifies, yet one that, as well as being a home for Om Borei and her daughter, also accommodated a number of relatives. As the larger house replacing it continues to do.

This multi-occupancy is something that struck us when Om Borei invited us to see the new building, the year before our first round of interviews, at a time when it was still under construction. There seemed to be people everywhere: her daughter and her daughter's husband, their children, some more children, a cousin or uncle. We must have seen the previous "very small" house, indeed we probably went in, but I don't remember it. I know, however, that it stood on the same plot of land.

The new house is relatively imposing, and contrasts with the buildings around, which are all much lower and less solid. We thought it strange, at first, that Om Borei should have elected not to move. In our part of the world it is not a good idea to have the best house in the road. But, of course, this is her neighbourhood, she has lived here for a long time, it is where all her friends are. Its location just outside the Church compound is convenient for popping into Church or into the presbytery, and it is not too far from the town centre.

In the course of our earlier visit, Om Borei pointed out the most interesting features of the redevelopment, especially the new sit down toilet, which was not yet plumbed in. I thought it might discharge into the ground, but we have since learnt that beneath the houses lies a network of sewage pipes. In this respect, things are not as bad as I feared.

The new house strikes me as a testimony to Om Borei's determination and hard work and the cohesiveness of the family unit. Her daughter and son-in-law seem just as industrious and enterprising as she is. Thus, when we visited last year, they were making sandals in their spare time to supplement their income, with Om Borei happily pitching in. One cannot but be impressed by the family's wise management of the little money they earn, their ability to seize opportunities, and their desire to improve their standard of living. It has paid off: the finished house is very nice, with yellow walls, beige floor tiles, and a range of seats. As is customary, there are various pictures on the walls. One is a photo of Om Borei's mother, another shows a younger

Borei. Most of the rest are pictures of members of the clergy. This is not unusual in Catholic circles in Cambodia, although this type of display would seem odd in an English home. There is also a statue of the Virgin Mary, a small cross, posters with both the English and Khmer alphabets, as well as a grotto with more religious statues in a corner of the front garden.

As we leave, Michael and I turn to each other: "She has had a hard life", we say. We will say this a lot in the coming days.

MING LIN

———

Battambang, January 2015

We, that is to say Ming Lin, Michael, Chanthorn (our interpreter), and I, are sitting in the presbytery, in a reception room on the ground floor that serves both as dining room and lounge, a meeting place for priests, parishioners and visitors. It is a pleasant environment with pictures and pot plants. When we first came, visitors were received in a similar room on the first floor which you entered from an airy veranda overlooking the compound. The veranda had a few tables and chairs and was used as an overflow dining area, or when it was too stuffy inside. As the rest of the first floor is occupied by the priests' bedrooms, there was no communal area for the clergy to relax and chat. The only way for them to have privacy was to lock the door between the veranda and the dining room and they were reluctant to do that. It was therefore decided to create a reception room out of some of the offices on the ground floor and move the kitchen and the dining room downstairs.

The new dining room is larger than the previous one, with three big dining tables and some easy chairs arranged round a

THEN THE KHMER ROUGE CAME

coffee table. The new kitchen boasts modern cooking facilities, at least by Cambodian standards, with an island worktop in the middle of the room that makes it unnecessary to sit on the floor to prepare food, as is the custom in Cambodia, and as you had to do in the old kitchen. The new arrangements also have the advantage of being more convenient for those bringing in supplies: not only the food itself, sometimes for up to 15 or 20 people, but also the huge bottles of purified water that no longer require carrying upstairs. The current facilities undoubtedly represent an improvement over the former set up for those most concerned, but we miss the veranda with its vantage point over what was going on, and the relaxing sound of its wind chimes.

Ming Lin, our interviewee, has been employed as cook here for many years, and is a familiar figure to anybody who comes regularly to the presbytery. Everyone, including us, calls her Ming Lin, although we have discovered that this is not the correct form of address in our case. The students we teach in the evening laughed when we referred to her as Ming Lin: they can say that, but not us. You see, *Ming*, the first part of Ming Lin, means 'Auntie' and is the term you use to address a woman older than yourself; and Ming Lin isn't older than us. The thing is that when you first go to Cambodia you have no idea of the intricacies of Khmer terms of address. You hear other people calling the cook Ming Lin so you copy them and say Ming Lin, and it may be quite some time before it dawns on you that this may not be how you should address her.

So what term should we use? Well this is rather tricky, even if it may not seem so at first. After all, it is not that difficult to grasp the idea that Khmer terms of address vary according to the gender of the person you are talking to and the age difference between you. Beware: this nutshell description is deceptive. The gender division is easy enough: there is one series for talking to males and another for talking to females and you can usually tell which category the person you are talking to belongs to (although it may not be obvious in the case of very old or emaciated people). So far so good. But then comes the much harder issue of the age difference between you. We are not just talking here of determining whether you are speaking to someone younger than you, of the same age, or older than you. A lady older than you is not necessarily called 'Auntie'. For Ming/Auntie to be the correct term, she needs to be both older than you *and* younger than your mother and father. Not young enough, mind you, to be called elder sister. I will spare you the whole gamut of possibilities. However, I should point out that there are sometimes simpler alternatives to the aunt, uncle, grandfather, etc. series, such as using a person's profession, for instance *Lok Kroo* (teacher) when talking to a male teacher.

How do you know how old someone is? Simple: if in doubt, ask. You will probably object that you can't do that, that you wouldn't dream of it, that it would be rude. It is indeed a taboo question in the West, a question out of the question, and I grant you that it takes time getting used to, whichever end of the question you happen to be on. But this is Cambodia and people do it all the time in order to make sure that they are addressing someone they don't know in the correct manner. If you can't bring yourself to ask people how old they are, if it really goes against the grain, then you will have to guess. Here, take into account that estimating the age of someone with different facial features than those you are used to is not unproblematic, so err on the side of caution. Which – and this will almost certainly come as a surprise – does not mean taking a few years off your best guess but the opposite: in Cambodia age commands respect, so give the person you are talking to the benefit of a few extra years.

If all this threatens to put you off ever talking to a Cambodian person, bear in mind that Cambodians are wonderfully tolerant and that they won't expect you to master all these niceties on your first visit. By the end of which you will have imitated those around you, and, in Om Lin/Ming Lin's case, you will have become accustomed to calling her Ming Lin, blissfully ignorant that this may not be the right way of addressing her. In case you are wondering, strictly speaking, we should call Ming Lin *Paon Srei* (younger sister), but it would not feel natural, and she is happy with *Ming*.

Ming Lin has a way of greeting visitors warmly which makes it a joy to see her. When we arrive in the morning, she and I usually have a little hug, followed by the traditional "How are you?", one of the bits of conversation I can manage in Khmer. Ming Lin does not speak English but over the years she has picked up a number of words and phrases from visitors. She seems to have an ear for languages and her pronunciation and intonation are almost flawless. Her "party piece", which she picked up from a long term American volunteer, is "Oh my God!" and she gladly parades this to everyone's merriment, including her own.

She is a brilliant cook. Not only are the dishes she prepares extremely tasty, but she is not the kind of person fazed by the sudden arrival of unexpected guests. She makes a point of spoiling people and will rustle up something nice in no time. In recent years, we have tended to take our evening meals in the Tep Im Centre rather than in the presbytery. The Centre is a student hostel subsidised by the Church and by private donations that enables young people from poor families, both Catholic and Buddhist, to come to Battambang to pursue their studies. The students are provided with meals (which they cook) and accommodation (which they are responsible for cleaning) and, if necessary, are given financial help with university fees and other expenses. They are not bad at cooking, but what they produce is not up to Ming Lin's standards. Ming Lin knows this and insists on bringing us a little treat, often a salad of some kind. We can protest as much as we like that she does not have to, she just goes ahead. Resigning ourselves – and, if truth be told, actually quite grateful – we share these titbits with the students who happen to be sitting at our table, who clearly appreciate them as much as we do.

It is early afternoon. Lunch is over. Ming Lin has come to join us and we are all sitting comfortably in easy chairs around the coffee table. There is a cool breeze flowing through the room. And I am totally, totally, unprepared for what I am about to hear.

Ming Lin begins by telling us that she is 63 and that she was the second of four children. Are all her siblings still alive? I enquire. "No", she replies, her two brothers died during the Khmer Rouge regime, one in 1976 and the other in 1979, shortly before the arrival of the Vietnamese. In 1973, her elder brother, who was a nurse and 12 years her senior, had fallen in love with the daughter of a friend of their father's and had got married. The couple were to die within two months of each other not long afterwards, the wife in childbirth, the husband executed by the Khmer Rouge after being accused of acting as an interpreter for the US – the standard punishment for those regarded as having been associated with the enemy. The other brother, who was younger than Ming Lin, had served as a soldier under Lon Nol. Ming Lin was working in a Youth Camp at the time of his death and she does not know the exact circumstances. She puts his death down to his family ties with the elder brother, but maybe his involvement with the army of the previous regime eventually came to light and the Khmer Rouge decided he should be got rid of.

Ming Lin has told us that the family were Buddhist, that her father was an army doctor, and that her mother looked after the house. Given her background, I am surprised to hear her say that she can't really read and is even less able to write. But, she explains, her father's job meant that the family was constantly on the move and this interfered with her education. Ironically, she owes her limited literacy skills to the Khmer Rouge, who taught her the little that she knows.

Like so many of her compatriots, Ming Lin was forced by the Khmer rouge to go and work in the fields, in her case in the vicinity of Battambang. Elaborating on what this experience was like, she will explain in a subsequent interview that she was assigned to a team that was tasked with carrying soil for the construction of a dam. The whole team lived near the workplace, exposed to the elements, the girls in a hut, the boys outside. She relates how everything would get wet when it rained and how they would all have to eat in the rain. How they would go in the river to try and keep warm when the weather was cold and windy. How all they ever ate was *bobor*, a kind of rice porridge, adding that they never had steamed rice, vegetables or meat and that everything was supposed to be common property. Should someone come by an edible banana or happen to catch a fish, he, or she, would have to share this with the others. She tells us how they were liable to be woken up at 2 or 3 am at harvest time and sent to help with the harvesting. And to top it all, talking at work was strictly forbidden. It was a life of shocking servitude hemmed in by endless restrictions, a kind of solitary confinement without walls spent toiling away at the mercy of those in control. It had descended upon her one day, just like that, and would go on for over three years. Relentlessly. Day after day.

After day.

Unbelievably, worse was in store for her, a dreadful development that would impact the rest of her life in the form of an "official", unsolicited and unwelcome marriage proposal from one of the men working in the same camp. She turned him down. Another marriage proposal came her way, followed by a third. Of course, Ming Lin does not have any photos from that period but a few days after the interview, she brings us a picture taken later on which gives a pretty good idea of what she must have looked like in those days. When you look at the picture, it is not hard to understand why men were attracted to her.

Then came a fourth proposal. She did not like or love the fourth suitor any more than any of the other three and did not want to marry him either. But the Khmer Rouge were keen to encourage procreation. Aware that she had already refused three proposals, they issued her with an ultimatum: "Marry the man or …" She knew what the "or" meant and she did not want to die.

The wedding ceremony was a communal affair, for 27 couples, 10 of whom had opted to marry, albeit sometimes under duress like Ming Lin. The other 17 couples were forced to marry against their will. The couples held hands and were proclaimed married. They were given a house, one per couple, and expected to "get on with it", as Ming Lin puts it euphemistically. Whether they liked it or not. And if, after a week, the spies sent by the Khmer Rouge to crawl under the house and listen for evidence still reported that you were not "getting on with it", you were killed. Typically, the wife, presumed to be the guilty party, would be taken away and hit on the back of the head with a shovel, possibly because it saved ammunition. "After a week, it was too late", Ming Lin adds. Her fate had been sealed.

The couple's first child was born in 1978 in the house they had been allocated. They were to have six more children, two of whom have since died: one of their sons died after falling from a tree in which he was picking fruit to sell, and a daughter succumbed to an unspecified illness at the age of two.

For most of their married life, Ming Lin's husband drank and beat her for the flimsiest of reasons. By the time the Vietnamese arrived and liberated them, she knew full well what he was like. People advised her to divorce him, but, she says, she did not want her child to have two fathers. Tears roll down her face as she recounts how when he was inebriated, her husband would hit her and would deprive her of food if she came back late from work. She would be so afraid at times that she would go and sleep at a neighbour's.

Observing her distress, on the verge of tears myself, I worry about the effect that the interview is having on her. I offer to stop. She does not want to stop, she wants to carry on: "I want to tell my story", she says. So I just lean over and squeeze her hand. I try to think of a way of lightening the mood. Recalling that Ming Lin and I have enjoyed showing each other pictures of our respective grandchildren, I ask about the happiest period in her life, expecting her to say "Now". But she doesn't. She has had to borrow money for repairs to her house and is worried about the repayments. She also worries about her children. No, the happiest period of her life was when she was living with her parents, before Pol Pot, before her marriage.

I find this terribly sad.

THE BRIGHTER SIDE

———

Battambang

The hotel we stay at in Battambang is called the Rattanak. We did patronize another hotel some years ago when Fr Pedro persuaded us to go upmarket. "You'll be more comfortable there", he told us. We were, physically. There were plush carpets on the floors and an attractive looking swimming pool. How nice the swimming pool was, or how clean, I can't say, as we never ventured in. Breakfast was the ubiquitous Western-style hotel breakfast, good and plentiful. But it did not feel right to enjoy this level of luxury when we were seeing so much poverty every day, and the reaction of the Tep Im students who happened to be in the pick-up truck when we were dropped off at our hotel one evening, their surprised exclamations: "Is that where you are staying?", did nothing to dispel our disquiet. The following year, we went back to the Rattanak.

Apart from providing accommodation we are congruent with, that is to say ensuite facilities and air conditioning but no frills, the main advantage of the Rattanak is its convenient location. A mere five to ten minutes walk from the church compound, it allows us to come and go as we please without having to call a tuk-tuk. No significant improvements or updating perceptible to the naked eye appear to have been carried out since our first stay, but we know from the makeshift repairs they have done in the various rooms we have had over the years that they fix leaks and other major issues. This of course does not stop the facilities from deteriorating year on year and the appearance of the rooms leaves quite a lot to be desired. But it is a familiar environment, and as valued customers we are greeted warmly when we arrive.

They kind of speak English. We are not talking great fluency and extensive vocabulary. Just basic, somewhat quirky English. As exemplified by the English version of the menu the ground floor restaurant used to hand out, out of consideration for the few foreigners brave enough to have breakfast there. The restaurant has now moved up the road, though not upmarket, to a converted garage a few doors away, where it offers customers the same menu with an improved but less endearing translation.

Here is an account of breakfast at the Rattanak from an email I sent Michael in August 2008 when I went to Cambodia on my own:

Fancied tea and bread but neither to be seen on the menu, which had the usual fare of noodle soup etc. plus a lot of dishes I had never heard of. Like "lette".

Was getting down to close scrutiny when waitress, leaning over me, helpfully suggested omelette, pointing at an item which read

"Ome lette break"

This seemed a good idea so I ordered "Ome lette break", together with orange juice, to be brought first, and coffee with milk.

Waitress sauntered away only to come back a couple of minutes later:

"Ome lette break no"

By then I quite fancied omelette, but such things happen. Ever helpful, she pointed at the line above

"Fried eggs break"

adding: "Eggs yes"

I was totally mystified. Brain frantically trying to recall how you make an omelette. No help there.

Still, fried eggs was OK so I ordered

"Fried eggs break please"

The response was immediate

"Fried eggs break no"

I could not believe the cruelty of the woman, dangling prospects before me only to take them away when I ordered.

She spotted that we had a communication problem. So, finger on "break" in "Ome lette break":

"Break no"

Moving down the menu and covering "break" in "fried eggs break"

"Break no"

… The problem was obviously with "break" and it looked as if I might get my omelette after all

"I'll have an omelette then please"

She looked concerned

"Ome lette break no"

I reassured her:

"Break no"

And so, a few minutes later, I was given first coffee (of course), followed by butter and marmalade, orange juice and omelette. I sent the butter and marmalade back for what use are butter and marmalade without break?

The limited English of the staff, including those manning the reception desk, is not without benefits. Sure, it can occasionally prove a problem, but, on the other hand, it gives us a chance to practise our Khmer and spurs us on to expand our vocabulary. For instance, it has provided us with the opportunity to learn how to say "cockroach" in Khmer, a term ignored by our textbooks. We had dutifully learnt how to say "Is there a bank nearby?" and "Could I have the menu please?" but had not had the chance to master the arguably more useful "There is a cockroach in my room". Not, let me hasten to add, that I think the authors were in any way remiss, or worse, were intentionally concealing the possibility of spotting a cockroach in your hotel for fear of deterring prospective visitors. It is just that the target readership they had in mind stayed in classier establishments *sans* cockroaches.

I have to confess that I know so little about wild life that when I saw a blackish beastie crawl out from under the shower when I was by myself in August 2008, I panicked. I knew it wasn't a spider, it was too fat for that, but what was it? I went to get one of the cleaners and, pointing to the gap under the shower, tried to mime a crawling insect coming out. She seemed quite amused but not too bothered, so I mentioned it to one of the missionaries. Was it a scorpion? He didn't think so. Reassured, I just got used to switching the bathroom light on before gingerly opening the door. The cockroach wasn't of the sociable type and would hastily retreat under the shower when I went in. I found this most considerate and resigned myself to having a shared bathroom.

Like any living thing, cockroaches have preferences and seem to us to favour certain rooms, which we are only too happy to leave to them. An amicable arrangement suiting both parties. Until broken. In 2015 we found an intruder in our room. And not anywhere in the room, not venturing cautiously from underneath the shower, but ensconced on the wall next to my bed. Quite another thing, if you intend to sleep in the bed. Action was needed. We marched down to reception and attempted to describe our problem. They were most sympathetic and soon produced a can of mosquito spray. At which point the desirability of knowing how to say "cockroach" in Khmer hit us. As our dictionary was no help, we attempted to illustrate the difference between mosquitoes and cockroaches with gestures and appropriate sound effects, at least as far as the first species was concerned. We had a go at drawing a cockroach, a pretty desperate measure when you consider how bad we are at drawing. Nothing worked. The receptionist listened patiently, completely nonplussed. In the end she decided, quite wisely, to get someone to take a look.

There followed the most epic chase you ever saw, with the young man whom the receptionist had sent to investigate leaping athletically on and off my bed while the cockroach tried its best to escape. Vainly, as it turned out. Let Man rule over all the beasts of the earth including cockroaches on walls. End of story. But a nagging doubt remained. Was it really the end? Was the adventurous cockroach a lone globetrotter or had it been sent, perhaps, on a reconnaissance mission? We decided to play it safe and changed our minds about the spray. Sensing the gravity of the situation, our gallant rescuer was most liberal in his fumigation duties. This worried us. If the spray killed everything, as the picture on the can seemed to suggest, what was it going to do to us? Still it worked. The matter was closed, but we thought it prudent to learn the word for cockroach. Just in case.

We spend quite a bit of time in Battambang helping the Tep Im students practise their English. In return, they have taught us bits of colloquial Khmer: "See you tomorrow", "Good night", "Sleep well", phrases that come in handy when we pick up our room key in the evening. Unless, of course, the receptionist happens to be sleeping on the job, as on a recent occasion. Leaning against the desk, with his head resting on his arms. "Could we please have our key?" we enquired. Oblivious to the world, the young night manager continued with his impersonation of Sleeping Beauty. Tapping him on the arm was more successful in making him stir, but he then swiftly returned to the Land of Nod. We were considering more serious measures, raising our voice, shaking him up, when a second tap on the arm finally did the trick. Rousing himself, he drowsily fumbled for our key and handed it over. Never one to miss an opportunity to use his Khmer, Michael could not resist showing off the remarkable extent of our repertoire of farewell formulae. "*Soben la'aw*" (sweet dreams), he wished mister heavy-eyed, as we were starting towards our room. A sheepish grin briefly flickered on the poor man's face.

OM REN

———

Battambang, January 2015

The venue for Om Ren's interview is neither her house, which we have visited in the past, nor the presbytery, but Fr Pedro's office in the Tep Im Centre. The presbytery is probably more comfortable, but Fr Pedro's office affords more privacy.

Situated opposite the presbytery, the Centre consists of a set of low buildings forming a quadrangle around a leafy garden. Fr Pedro's office is at the back. It is small and sparsely furnished with a desk, a couple of cupboards, some rattan chairs of the kind found in English conservatories, and a stack of old printers which he hopes to have repaired one day and can't bring himself to part with.

Om Ren arrives with three of her grandchildren in tow. The grandchildren listen in at first, but then lose interest and wander off to go and play in the garden, where we will join them for a photo at the end of the interview. All three, we are told, are currently living with her.

Om Ren is another of the Battambang ladies we have known for a long time. Her determined attempts to communicate with us in English made her stand out from the rest. These endeavours were rarely successful as her English was self taught and her pronunciation highly idiosyncratic. Lacking recordings, all she had to go by was her personal interpretation of the supposedly "phonetic" transcription shown in her textbook, a less than optimal scenario. We tried hard to puzzle out what she was saying, consulting each other about what it might be, before finally admitting defeat. Undeterred, she would repeat what she had said in a louder voice. When she realized that this did not help, she adopted a different tactic. She started bringing her book along, leafing through it to point out which word or phrase she was saying. A laborious process, as you may well imagine, which took a lot of time but, on the other hand, was occasionally rewarded with success. You had to give her 10 out of 10 for effort. I have yet to meet a more shining example of a dedicated and resourceful language learner. She just lacked a congenial learning environment.

One year, we noticed that she wasn't around. Not only when we arrived, but the next day, and the next, and the next. She was not attending Mass and was nowhere to be seen. She seemed to have vanished. We wondered whether she had died and people had forgotten to tell us, so we enquired after her. No, she had not died, she wasn't ill. She wasn't even too busy to come to Mass. She was ashamed. Ashamed? Of what? Ashamed because her youngest daughter, who suffers from a mental disability, had gone out one night, had become pregnant, and had given birth to a baby boy. It took several months for Om Ren to reappear. Sadly, the little boy, one of the three children accompanying her, is developmentally disabled and although the mother lives with Om Ren, the task of bringing him up falls mostly on his grandmother.

Om Ren's family is in many ways a kind of microcosm of family relationships in the area. Now a widow, she has had eleven children, eight of whom are still alive. One child died in 1979 after catching measles at the age of five. Another died the following year at the age of ten from an ailment akin to Dengue fever, a mosquito borne disease which stills kills many children in Cambodia. A third died later on from drug addiction.

Seven of her eight children live in Cambodia: two are in Battambang, three are in Phnom Penh, and the other two live near the Thai border. The eighth is in Thailand. They do a variety of jobs from selling cars, through hotel work, to teaching. Two, one of them the mother of the two girls she has come with, are divorced. Some send her money, though sometimes sporadically. Her main source of support is the Australian husband of one of her daughters, a not uncommon state of affairs around here.

As we were making our way to Om Ren's house on an earlier visit, we were greeted by a handicapped man sitting nearby on the side of the road. We asked Om Ren who the man was. Pointing to a little shack behind her house she replied that he lived there. He was not a relative, just a disabled person with no one to look after him, so she had given him this hut to sleep in and she also brought him food.

Asked about her childhood, she explains that she was born in 1947 in Chatiel, near Battambang, and was the eldest of four children. Her parents were farmers. Not rice farmers like most Cambodian farmers; they grew crops such as oranges and cabbages and sold them to others to take to market. When she was young, Om Ren used to help by working in the fields, for instance picking beans. She attended the local government school for three years and then worked in Phnom Penh selling oranges until she was 23. She married a builder from Battambang who was Catholic, converted to Catholicism, and started cooking and selling rice.

Like everyone else, the family was displaced when the Khmer Rouge took over Battambang. She was sent with the children to a nearby village called Ta Hen. There she worked in the fields again, this time harvesting rice. The older children were also made to work, while the others studied. Her husband had been appointed group leader in another place, where he had been put in charge of cooking rice. On discovering that she was pregnant, she asked the authorities to bring him back. She tells us how they did not take her word for it, but sent a man to investigate whether she was really pregnant. She does not spell out what the investigation involved.

The story progresses. You can tell from her voice, her general manner, the quickening of the overall pace, that we are reaching a momentous event, a crisis point. It has something to do with an order given to her husband, seemingly out of the blue, to build an oven under pain of death within two weeks. She does not offer any clue as to the reason for this extraordinary demand, and there is no chance to ask, for she has moved on to trying to convey the terror that seized them, the pressure he was under, and her own dread that he might fail and be executed since he did not know how to build ovens. She relates that she prayed silently, in her heart, for nearly a week, using a rosary she had kept despite the ban on religious practice, while he did his best to comply. Thankfully, he did manage to build an oven within the deadline, but the memory of the overwhelming anguish she felt during that traumatic episode will stay with her for ever.

When the Vietnamese arrived and started making enquiries about what had happened under Pol Pot, Om Ren and her husband took fright. Afraid that he might be arrested, they packed their goods on a bicycle, and set off on foot with their family towards the Thai border.

As she evokes her life in the refugee camp they settled in, she makes reference to people whose names we recognize, such as Sister Ath. When we met Sister Ath, she was in charge of the Health Centre run by the prefecture for people in need of basic treatments. She also held weekly clinics in the local prison and we accompanied her a couple of times. I can remember her fretting on one of those occasions as we stood waiting for the Spanish doctors who were coming with us to treat the inmates, anxious not to waste a minute of the short time slot allocated by the prison authorities. We only learnt later that Sister Ath was one of a very small number of Khmer nuns to have escaped the genocide, having gone to France to train as a nurse at the time of the Khmer Rouge takeover.

She would come back in 1987 to work with the Jesuit Refugee Service on the Cambodian border. We happened to be in Battambang when she died of cancer in France in December 2010. As is the custom here in such cases, the church bell was rung, announcing death and calling people to Mass. We were struck by the impact the news of her passing had on the community, by the visible grief surrounding us, unaware, as we then were, that some parishioners had made Sister Ath's acquaintance in the grim context of life in a refugee camp.

We do not catch the name of the camp Om Ren went to, but she tells us that they stayed there for 13 years before finally returning to Battambang in 1992. Her husband became a member of the camp's Catholic committee and taught catechism; she went back to cooking and selling rice; the children went to school.

They moved to where Om Ren now lives soon after their return. She explains how elections were held, how one of her sons helped with organising the process, and how everyone was given $50. Om Ren and her husband used their $50 to buy a bit of land and build a house. But there was to be no happy ending. A year later, her husband died from hepatitis. She herself fell ill with tuberculosis. She tells us that she needed three series of treatment, adding that Om Borei, our first interviewee, helped her with money. On more than one occasion in the course of our conversation with Om Borei, Om Borei's daughter, Magkara, intervened to remind her mother that she had helped people. It was a subject she clearly wanted her mother to expand on, but her remarks were brushed away, leaving an uncomfortable question mark in my mind. This unsolicited confirmation of Om Borei's willingness to come to her friends' aid sets my mind at peace.

"But what will happen to my grandchildren when I die?" Om Ren asks, at the end.

OM RI

Battambang, February 2015

What comes to my mind when I think of Om Ri is not anything she said in the course of the interview but an incident that took place three days later. Not that the interview was unmemorable. With hindsight, I should have been prepared for what happened, but I had not completely taken in the implications of what she had told us, so that the incident still eclipses our conversation in my memory.

I was sitting in the presbytery with the door open when, quite by chance, I spotted someone dragging a handcart loaded with rubbish across the compound. Hardly a minute goes by in the presbytery without someone passing in the vicinity. I might not have given the scene a second thought, except that the lady pulling the cart looked vaguely familiar. Suddenly, a light went on. It was one of those occasions when you do a double take, when you think: "No it can't be...", and look again. I rushed out to check that I was not mistaken, but did not manage to catch up with her before she reached her destination: a small recycling centre, hardly larger than a garage, 50 metres or so

60

down the road that borders the church compound. She had put the handles of the cart down and was standing next to it with a young girl by her side, waiting patiently to be attended to, while the guys in the sorting centre carried on with more important jobs. And yes, it was Om Ri.

I was aghast. Despite our long acquaintance, in the course of which we had seen her sweeping the drive as we arrived at the compound, despite what she had told us three days earlier about her financial situation, I had no idea that she had to supplement her earnings by selling rubbish picked up in the

streets or collected around the compound. It is difficult to find words to describe my emotions, not only at the time but also now, when I visualise the scene and reflect upon Om Ri's fate. What predominates is a feeling of sadness that she should have to live from scavenging, but there is also admiration and respect for her resourcefulness and hard work, for her dedication to her family.

And always the same unanswerable question lurking behind: "Why? Why her and not me?"

When the man in charge eventually turned his attention to her, Om Ri started unloading what was in the cart: bags full of cans and plastic bottles that were duly weighed on scales nearby. There followed some complex form filling. Cambodians adore filling

in forms. Even though what they write down isn't necessarily a faithful reflection of the deal entered into, and so provides no guarantee of everything being above board to outsiders – "What would like me to put on the receipt?" is not an unheard-of question – the mere existence of paperwork gives the transaction a degree (or semblance) of respectability. After Om Ri had approved the figures, the cashier produced a bundle of banknotes – Cambodia does not use coins, only paper money – from which Om Ri extracted a couple of notes for her little companion. She did tell me later what the goods had fetched. Even showed us the receipt. I can't recall the exact sum, but it can't have been much.

Om Ri had made no reference whatsoever to her recycling activities during the interview. Indeed, she had not made much of her poverty. She took poverty for granted. It was one of those facts of life. Certainly not what worried her most. Her main worry was her health.

There is a moment at the beginning of an interview while everyone is settling down, when the interviewee may seize the floor and share some concern that is preying on their mind. This happened several times over the three years we conducted interviews, and, more often than not, the concern was health related. I don't think these references to ill-health were made with any underlying expectation that we would help, perhaps pay for treatment, or know of a miracle cure. It was just that the issue was uppermost in the person's mind.

Almost the first things that Om Ri mentions, when we get together for the interview, is that she suffers from high blood pressure. She is 68 years old and all her siblings have passed away. One brother was killed in 1980 when "Pol Pot" – by which she means the Khmer Rouge – threw a bomb into a group of Vietnamese he worked for as a translator. Another brother died in 1991 from a blood pressure related illness. There is a family history of diabetes. In the past few months, she has lost both her sisters to fatal heart attacks and her mother, who died in 1994, suffered from high blood pressure. As she will tell us later, Om Ri herself had a stroke six years ago that left her unable to speak for three months. She is worried. She has been prescribed medication to lower her blood pressure, but, contrary to what happens in the UK in such cases, the State does not supply her with free medicine. Admittedly, she usually gets the pills free of charge from the prefecture's health centre, but the provision of free or subsidised medicine represents a major drain on the Church's resources, so she occasionally has to pay.

When we get on to the story of her life, Om Ri explains that her parents were farmers, but that her mother also worked for the Providence Sisters, helping to cook five or six huge bowls of rice for the patients being cared for in the hospital. She attended school from the age of 10 until she was 20, learning not only Khmer but also Vietnamese. Under Lon Nol, she followed in her mother's footsteps and worked as a cook, alongside Om Ren, our previous interviewee, in the morning, and then worked in the fields in the afternoon. Suddenly, Om Borei makes an unexpected appearance in the narrative: "Om Borei helped with husks of rice", she volunteers, without elaborating. I am amazed. Not by Om Borei's kindness, which is by now an established fact. Or even the length of time that Om Borei and Om Ri have known each other. What I find astonishing is the thought of people such as Om Borei, Om Ren and Om Ri, spending most of their life in the same place, within a mere 100 metre circle from one another. This is so unlike my own experience and the experience of most of the people I know. And yet, on reflection, this was the norm in pre-industrial societies. For all I know, taking the world as a whole, it may still be the case that more people remain near their place of birth than move away.

Om Ri has one child, a son, whom, like Om Borei, she has had to bring up on her own, though this is where the resemblance ends. Her husband did not disappear like Om Borei's did. He was a soldier in Lon Nol's army and, like so many others, was killed by the Khmer Rouge. It wasn't the first devastating blow to hit her. Five years earlier, she had married a man she had known since childhood, a union desired by her parents and also in line with the couple's feelings. However, having failed to conceive after four years of marriage, she was thought to be barren and her husband repudiated her. In one of those ironic twists of fate, it only took six months for her to become pregnant, when she married again. Tragically, any hopes of happiness she might have entertained were then dashed by her husband's death.

The child's birth was a protracted affair with contractions lasting three days. To my surprise, Om Ri mentions that the baby was delivered by a doctor, whom she describes as "not Pol Pot". If this means that the doctor had qualified before the Khmer Rouge takeover, he (or she) was taking a huge risk: to reveal that you belonged to the loathed professional classes was tantamount to signing your own death warrant.

Om Ri, who was living by herself at the time of the birth, was then joined by her mother, who came over to look after the baby, while her daughter worked in the rice fields. Following the defeat of the Khmer Rouge in 1979, Om Ri returned to Battambang, where she earned a living sewing clothes. I presume that this did not generate enough income because, after 18 months, she decided, for reasons she does not explain, to set off for Thailand with her mother-in-law, leaving her son in her sister's care. She came back in 1983. Her son moved back with her, and she worked once more as a seamstress, until her failing eyesight forced her to give up sewing and ask the Church for a job.

As expected from women of her generation, Om has spent a lot of time caring for relatives. When one of her nephews was orphaned, she took him in and brought him up. Before her son moved away, she took care of her grandchildren for 4 years. These days, she looks after a sister-in-law unable to cook for herself. And in a further demonstration of the importance of family bonds, she visits her younger sister's son in prison. The mother, her sister, died a fortnight after her son's incarceration, and Om Ri has taken on going to see him three times a month. She says he has a drug addiction and was accused of selling drugs, although, according to her, there is no proof that he did.

Om Ri's is a particularly punishing schedule. Her day begins at 5 am when she gets up to cook breakfast. At 6 am she goes to Mass and then goes to the market to buy food for lunch. People don't have fridges or freezers here, so fresh food has to be purchased daily. From 7.30 to 9.30 she sweeps and cleans the grounds in the church compound. She then goes home to prepare lunch for herself and her sister-in-law, before taking what she has cooked to her sister-in-law's home. She has a rest, then goes back to work for another three hours. She cooks dinner, takes this to her sister-in-law's, and they eat together.

"What is the best, happiest time of your week?" I ask. "On Sunday, when I go to Mass", she replies.

OM PRANYA

—

Battambang, February 2015

Our fifth interviewee was a lady called Om Pranya. Om Pranya and I normally speak French to each other. She learnt French at school and is still very fluent. But telling her life story proved a step too far and she soon switched to her native tongue.

Om Pranya is the type of person who is the life and soul of the party. Outgoing, lively, articulate and funny, she is a true extrovert. I remember a parish amateur variety show she appeared in during one of our early visits, in which she paced the stage in a humorous, self-mocking rendition of a coquette, playing to the audience, who all knew her. They loved it and roared with laughter.

Unlike Om Borei, Ming Lin, Om Ren and Om Ri, who all live on the East side of the church compound, Om Pranya lives on the relatively busy street that passes in front of it, on the North side. Houses here tend to be more substantial. Om Pranya's is a solid single story building with a side entrance reached via a narrow alleyway. Most dwellings along the road are fronted by small shops, from laundry services to food stalls. Om Pranya's isn't, but her husband was a tailor by trade and before he died in 2014, their front room doubled up as his workshop.

Since his death the room serves as a living room/bedroom. Opening straight onto the walkway it seems quite spacious, at first sight, by Cambodian standards. It also looks rather sparsely furnished. Both impressions are deceptive. The apparent spaciousness and the relative emptiness are due to the way the room is laid out. As is common practice, almost all the furniture is pushed right back against the walls, leaving a bare area in the middle, which chairs are dragged into when Om Pranya has visitors. There are many more things in the room than appear at first glance. In fact, if you look around you after settling into your seat, you will find yourself encircled by a motley collection of cupboards, chests of drawers, sideboards, small tables, as well as a pile of plastic garden chairs, a hammock, a bed. You will discover an equally diverse range of objects on all the horizontal surfaces, including some statues and crucifixes. You will note that most of the cabinets are full to overflowing, as if to demonstrate the endemic nature of people's storage issues.

The stark contrast between the empty centre and the cluttered periphery makes the middle appear under siege, and provides a vivid illustration of a desperate attempt – which many of us will sympathise with – to keep at bay the assault of every day living on aspirations to orderliness. Although the centre finds itself on the losing side when the chairs are set out, the invasion is temporary, as the chairs will be stacked up again when the visitors leave.

Unsurprisingly, given Om Pranya's reduced circumstances, the general décor is tired. The green tiled floor was obviously put in years ago, the walls could do with a lick of paint. But struggling as she does to cover her basic needs, she can ill afford to divert any of her meagre resources into internal decoration.

Despite her hand-to-mouth existence, she never fails, however, to switch on the electric fan hanging from the ceiling when we arrive. A considerate gesture which one would appreciate more, if the ceiling was not so low, and the fan a potential hazard. Michael forgot to duck sufficiently under it one year and nearly got himself decapitated.

When Om Pranya's husband was alive, the first thing you came across, on entering the alleyway to the side of the house, was a row of sewing machines. I remember visiting after he fell ill. It was a Saturday, or maybe a Sunday, and a couple of his daughters, who had jobs during the week, were busy making garments to help raise funds for his treatment. We have seen a prescription for the medicines he had to take. They came to $80 per week, a hefty sum in a country where $3 was not an uncommon daily wage, even if a tailor might be expected to earn a bit more. Besides impairing his ability to work, the illness had a crippling effect on the family's finances and his death left his widow with a $500 debt.

As if this was not bad enough, one of Om Pranya's daughters has been diagnosed with Hepatitis C, a treatable but costly disease. The daughter tries to support herself by doing some cleaning, selling fruit and working in restaurants, but she cannot meet the full medical costs of her treatment. In recognition of the services that Om Pranya has given the Church over the years, and of the help she continues to provide, she receives $125 per month to help with the payments, but when things are bad and her daughter's earnings drop, there is a shortfall.

To all appearances, Om Pranya and her husband got on well. As is the case for most women of that generation, the marriage was arranged by Om Pranya's parents without consulting her. When I ask her, during the interview, how she felt when she was informed of her parents' plans, she admits that she was not particularly happy. I ask whether she spoke to them about her feelings. Speak to them about her feelings? Of course not! The idea did not even cross her mind. It would have been unthinkable. Arranged marriages were the norm in those days and that was that. You complied, you did what you were told.

We were sitting opposite Om Pranya at lunch in the presbytery one day, about the time of the interview, when I got up to go and fetch some water. When I came back, Om Pranya was murmuring something to the missionary priest sitting next to her. During my absence from the table, some ginger tea had come round. Michael had helped himself and had also poured some tea into my cup. To us a routine gesture, but to Om Pranya a sign of attention and affection, and she had confided to the priest that she had never been treated like this. Not unnaturally, she felt a little envious. Hidden desires of the heart, unmet emotional needs, found everywhere, but so prevalent here.

Om Pranya was born and bred in Battambang. Unlike most local people, her parents were not farmers. Her father was a fisherman, her mother filleted the catch, smoked it and sold it. This meant that Om Pranya and her four siblings always had plenty of fish to eat, and therefore a much better diet, in all likelihood, than other children.

The youngest in the family, she studied with the Providence Sisters until the age of 17, when she started teaching. She began by taking care of foreign children to whom she taught French in the morning and Khmer in the evening, and then moved to a teacher assistant position. She stopped teaching when the Khmer Rouge seized power in 1975.

When she turns to what happened, Om Pranya gets very animated. There is a noticeable change in her manner, an accumulation of details, that are not just the trade mark of a born raconteur: she is talking about a dramatic, traumatic development, a series of momentous events that profoundly impacted her life and the lives of those around her, and are lodged deep in her memory. Born in 1945, she was 30 at the time, so has clear recollections of what took place, and the narration sweeps her back to that time.

The Khmer Rouge, she says, came into Battambang shooting. She was attending what would turn out to be Monsignor Tep Im's last Mass in Battambang. She describes how he blessed everyone, while the Khmer troops surrounded the building. She moves her hand and her head to illustrate how they circled round and round, watched by the congregation, who must have been terrified. The soldiers did not come in, but she would never see Mgr Tep Im again. In fact, it would be nearly 20 years before Battambang had another priest, as Catholic priests would not be permitted to come back until the full restoration of the right to worship freely in 1992.

Mgr Tep Im's plan was to take his parents to France and then return to Cambodia. He never did. He was killed at Bat Trang on his way to Thailand, together with Fr Jean Badré, a Benedictine monk who was the parish priest of Chomnaom at the time. Om Pranya explains that Mgr Tep Im's full name was Paul Tep Im Sotha. His mother was French and was called Marguerite, his father was Khmer. Tep was his grandfather's name, Im his father's name, Sotha his own first name. Paul was his Christian name. She adds that he was handsome, quiet spoken, and gentle. She liked him a lot.

Things soon got worse in Battambang. Announcing that the King was about to fly in – Battambang had an airport in those days – the Khmer Rouge ordered all the high ranking officers of Lon Nol's army, as well as a number of businessmen, to go and welcome him. It was a trap. The King was not scheduled to come to Battambang at all, and those who had gone to the airport to greet him never returned.

Forced out of Battambang with the rest of the population, Om Pranya and her husband were made to work in the rice fields. They found this very hard as they were not used to planting and harvesting rice and did not know what to do. They had three daughters by then, who would be taken away in the morning, while their parents went to the paddy fields.

Food became extremely scarce and, in 1977, Om Pranya's mother died of starvation. This was not Om Pranya's only loss during those bleak years, which were marked by brutal reprisals and the settling of scores. Only two of her four siblings survived the barbaric regime: her sister and a brother who had become a priest and had gone to France in 1967, where he would remain until his death in 1999. Her other two brothers belonged to the governmental army, and suffered the fate that befell most of Lon Nol's troops.

Unusually, when so many people try their luck outside Cambodia, none of Om Pranya's five children has left their homeland. Three of them actually live in Battambang city, earning a living by selling goods, by working in a public address business, or, in the case of her son, who provides her with some money, as a construction worker. She has grandchildren ranging in age from a few months to 27, and takes care of some of the younger ones from time to time.

Like virtually everyone else, Om Pranya tells us that the happiest period in her life was before she got married and acquired lots of responsibilities. She specifically mentions the good feelings she had singing in church at that time. Church, she says, continues to be a great source of pleasure for her as it takes her mind off her troubles. She enjoys being involved in preparing celebrations, and, more surprisingly, helping with funerals, when she stays with the bereaved family to offer them support.

One can see a pattern emerging, with the church serving not only as a liturgical centre, but also as a source of opportunities for collaborating with others over projects and activities that help provide a sense of fulfilment. It is a place where you go and pray, but it also gives you a chance to leave your problems behind for a time.

CHOMNAOM

We discovered some time ago that, contrary to what we assumed, the area surrounding Chomnaom church is not called Chomnaom, but Rong Vien. Rong Vien Lich (West) to be precise. According to Chanthorn, our interpreter, who should know since he comes from these parts, Chomnaom is the next village along the river, the last locality that you pass on your way to Rong Vien by car. Why is the church called Chomnaom church rather than Rong Vien church? One possible explanation is that as well as being the name of a village, Chomnaom is the name of the commune that encompasses Rong Vien and Chomnaom. In a similar way, the name Battambang is used to designate a city or a province. As it happens, Chomnaom is not located in Battambang province, but in Banteay Manchey province, so that the church's full address is St Therese of the Child Jesus church, Rong Vien village, Chomnaom commune, Mongkol Borei district, Banteay Manchey province. Quite a mouthful, but the sort of thing the Tep Im students rattle off when we ask them where they come from. Leaving us, needless to say, somewhat baffled and none the wiser.

The area hasn't always been the kind of backwater place it has become. It was once somewhere that people wanted to move to, attracted by the farming and fishing opportunities on offer. I don't know the complete history of the village, but the parish is said to have been created in 1910 under the French protectorate, when two Catholic families relocated here from Battambang. Others followed and a small church was built, to be replaced, as the community kept on growing, by something big enough to accommodate what remains to this day a relatively large number of Catholics. The influx does not seem to have caused animosity, and Catholics are said to have entertained good relations with their Buddhist neighbours.

This peaceful state of affairs was to come to an end with the rise in the late 1940s of the Khmer Issarak (Free Khmer), an anti-French nationalist movement backed by Thailand and made up of guerrilla factions operating independently. Originally non-communist, the Khmer Issarak linked up with the communist Viet Minh resistance movement fighting for Vietnam's independence from France. Catholics, perceived as betraying the Khmer nation because of their adherence to a religion different from the majority and associated with the French, became the victims of persecutions and killings. Vietnamese Catholics were particularly targeted, a typical example of ethnic cleansing (before the term became widespread). They would eventually leave the village, hence a considerably higher percentage of Khmer Catholics among the congregation than is the norm.

The gaining of independence in 1953, and the agreement reached at the Geneva Conference of 1954 to end the war in Indochina, marked the beginning of a period of relative peace for Cambodia that was to last for 16 years. But the Khmer communists were getting organized and would start launching sporadic attacks.

In a letter to his father written in February 1969, Fr Jean Badré, who has become Chomnaom's parish priest, refers to the presence of Khmer Rouge guerrillas in Battambang province, hastening to add that they are few in numbers and do not interfere with everyday life (Bourboulon, 2017). Maybe the father's mind was set at rest when he read that life was going on as usual, but the reassurance makes me shudder, knowing, as I do, that, six years later, Fr Badré will be executed by the Khmer Rouge, as he travels alongside Mgr Tep Im.

That the Buddhists and Catholics of Chomnaom are still on friendly terms is perhaps never more in evidence than at the blessing of the village, an annual Catholic ceremony consonant with the local Buddhist culture. One of the high points in the Chomnaom social calendar, it is one of those not-to-be-missed events. Unique to Chomnaom parish, it attracts Catholics from all around. It could take place without the bishop, but Bishop Kike likes to be there. It is therefore a moveable feast, subject to the moonlike influence of episcopal comings and goings. For in the grand scheme of things, an informal village festivity does not have quite the same kind of power over a bishop's diary as being invited to the Vatican, attending a bishops' conference, or even saying Mass in Battambang city on Easter Sunday.

There are other constraints to take into account. Clearly the village blessing cannot be held during the rainy season without losing much of its appeal and joyful atmosphere. Even the most committed of Catholics is unlikely to relish wading through inches of water on muddy dirt tracks, and you can hardly expect people to wait contentedly under torrential rain for the arrival of a procession. The harvest season is also out, as the villagers are busy gathering the crops. They are also busy at sowing time. All of which leaves a short window of opportunity in February/March, during the dry season, when not much else is happening.

I have heard the village blessing compared to a cross between a traditional blessing and a water fight. There is an element of truth in this description. The amount of water used is undeniably more copious than is the case in similar ceremonies in my part of the world and the general atmosphere is light hearted. Yet this does not interfere with the prayerful character of the blessings, which can be very moving, particularly if a sick or elderly person is involved.

Like many annual events, the village blessing has become ritualised and the proceedings follow a set pattern. The ceremonial part begins with Mass. Beforehand, the compound will have been festooned with red and white bunting and by mid-morning local parishioners are milling around, waiting for the visitors to arrive. "Is he there yet?" people ask. They mean Bishop Kike, the principal celebrant, who will be presiding over Mass. Clearly, nothing is going to happen until he is here. How many clergy will attend is uncertain, but he may well be joined at the altar by a dozen priests, who will make no attempt to rush back to their respective parishes after Mass, aware that it is only the first part of a unique festive occasion and that there is more to come. Mass over, the whole congregation will be served a delicious and plentiful meal in the parish grounds, a jolly interlude generously provided by the local community.

Then comes the part that – let's be honest – everyone has really come for: the actual village blessing. Four or five kojuns, the small versatile hand-tractors found throughout Cambodia, drive into the compound. They will not be used today in a paddy field or to transport ordinary commodities. Two of them will be pulling trailers with priests in white albs (vestments), standing or sitting with a jug in their hand, ready to scoop water out of large containers. The other kojuns will carry the sound system and its huge speakers, or some of the laity. It is clear that there will not be enough room for everyone, but that does not matter as many people, ourselves included, prefer to walk.

The general hubbub comes abruptly to an end with the sound of a drum roll calling people to gather in front of the church. A percussion band and a small dancing group will accompany the procession as it winds its way round the village. All the musicians and dancers are young and wear colourful traditional costumes. Part of the mission of the diocese is to promote Cambodian art and culture, and the village blessing

provides a chance to showcase the integration of Khmer culture into Catholic festivities.

The convoy sets off, each kojun leaving the compound to turn left along the road. It is the custom, if you wish to receive a blessing, to stand in front of your house with buckets full of water. So, dotted along the route every 30 metres or so, are little groups of people, usually family units, waiting to be focussed on and prayed over in turn. Beads in a human rosary laid out around the church that are looking for a few moments of individual attention from a priest whose faith they do not necessarily share. An encounter imbued with mutual respect, symbolic of a relationship made visible through the pouring of water which, when it catches the light, ceases to be mere droplets to take on the appearance of a descending shimmering halo.

Outside this private oasis of peace, there is chatting, music, dancing, as participants move around, take pictures, jump on or off the kojuns, and try to splash each other. It is fun to watch, it is nice to be among people enjoying life, to be part of it all. And

to know that should it get too much for you, you can step out of all the jollity, and come up for a blessing yourself. You will get wet, for the priests do not hold back when they pour water on your head, but then you are probably soaked already, and anyway clothes dry quickly in this heat.

In the absence of tourist accommodation, our first visits to Chomnaom were limited to day trips. However, by the time of our first interviews, we had graduated to staying overnight. Now, the Rattanak may not be a five-star hotel, but it still provides rather more creature comforts than the sleeping quarters of Chomnaom church, three rooms on the upper floor of the administrative block: a bedroom for the priest when he stays over in Chomnaom, a small dormitory for some of the Tep Im students who come to help at the weekend – the others go to their family home or to their friends' – and a guest room.

Although of a higher standard than most of the houses in the vicinity, the accommodation is somewhat basic: wooden beds made of slats with a thin mattress on top – admittedly a step up from the rush mats most people sleep on; ensuite with a cold shower and a sit-down toilet next to what looks like an unemptied bath, but is actually a cistern complete with jug for DIY toilet flushing, and, in the place of air conditioning, electric fans that you refrain from switching on, knowing this will increase the electricity bill. The bedrooms do offer a degree of privacy, but to let the air circulate and make them less stifling, the windows are unglazed and the top of the partitions dividing the space up have gaps in them. Letting not just air through, but also light and the slightest sound. So you tiptoe around, mindful of your neighbours, and considerately turn off your light if you notice they've turned theirs off.

With a bit of luck silence falls – apart, that is, from the odd mosquito circumnavigating your mosquito net – and reigns for a little while. Long enough, anyway, to lure you to sleep. While all around, unseen, are all manners of animals – dogs, cockerels, etc. – eager to exercise their voice and stake a claim on the jungle surrounding you. Repeatedly, if need be. Noise travels a long way in open environments and unglazed windows offer no protection, so the chances of a good night's sleep are virtually nil. That is not all: when you have managed to doze off again for the nth time, you may well be abruptly woken up, not at the crack of dawn – that would not be so bad – but actually before, by music or announcements transmitted over a PA system (public address system). It is a fairly safe bet that should this occur, your first reaction won't be one of delight. Music, announcements, at this hour, without regard to those trying to sleep? But the concept of antisocial noise is culture bound and unfamiliar to most people here. Moreover, there is a point to this seemingly outrageous disturbance. Like church bells before Mass, or the call to prayer from a minaret, it serves to remind local people of the imminence of a significant event or obligation: a wedding they may have been invited to, a funeral they ought to attend. By the way, this is only the start. The music and announcements are not going to stop any time soon. They will probably continue, interspersed with hope-inducing, all too brief silences, for a good few hours, all day perhaps. Like heat, it is another of those aspects of life in rural Cambodia that you don't see on a photo.

YIEY KOUM

———

Chomnaom, February 2015

We are on our way to Yiey Koum's home. As is often the case
in the countryside, most of the plots here are bigger than in
Battambang. As a result, the houses are set further apart. The
larger ones have a fruit and vegetable garden, as well as a few
outbuildings: toilets, a separate kitchen, a couple of sheds, some
shelters for animals. The smaller ones don't.

Nothing distinguishes the place where Yiey Koum lives
from its neighbours. A medium size dwelling with a first floor
and a sitting area below, it seems quite spacious for someone
at her stage of life, but I guess this is where her children were
brought up. It is better than some of the habitations we have
come across, but not grand, an average family house. There is
nothing special about Yiey Koum's appearance either, but what
she says when she begins talking about her early life reveals a
comparatively affluent background with the kind of standard of
living only found among rural families better off than average.

Like almost all the other interviewees, when I ask her what
has been the happiest time in her life, she replies that she was

happiest before her marriage, when she was still a child. But, tellingly, what she focuses on are the material advantages of that period: "My father had lots of fields, we had money, food, a big house." "What happened to the house?" I ask. "It was demolished by the Khmer Rouge." "Did the Khmer Rouge pull down all the houses?" "No", she replies, "only the big ones." No-one in Battambang mentioned their house – or anyone else's for that matter – being pulled down. Is it an omission of no special significance, something they neglected to tell us, or is it that more houses were destroyed in the rural areas? Were the larger houses more likely to be taken down, as Yiey Koum claims, and if so, why? This is our first Chomnaom interview, we'll have to find out.

Progress is painfully slow. Most of my questions are followed by a long silence, without any clear sign that a reply is forthcoming. Whereas other people make eye contact, Yiey Koum sits staring ahead with a blank look on her face, in a daze, as if she is not entirely "with it". We are sitting in the open area under her house, in surroundings that are familiar to her, but she seems disoriented, lost. I have been told that she was widowed recently and I put her behaviour down to her being in a state of shock, still grieving for her husband, lonely and depressed by her new circumstances. Her daughter, who has come to sit beside her – another of those uninvited guests, although, in this case, one whose presence I welcome – tries to move things along, repeating the questions and occasionally chipping in. I wonder whether she came to join us because she anticipated there might be difficulties. We press on, as best we can.

"Yes, I did", Yiey Koum replies, when I enquire whether she learnt to read and write. Unusually, for someone from the countryside, especially a girl, she spent a year as a boarder with the Providence Sisters in Battambang, in-between working in her parents' fields. Her parents, she says, sold some of their rice to support her education, another sign of relative affluence.

She goes on: "I learnt, but I have forgotten." A bizarre assertion, that may seem hard to believe. Except that the Khmer script is anything but straightforward, and it is conceivable that, without regular practice, someone may indeed cease to be able to read and write. Just as there are documented instances of people losing their ability to speak their native tongue after emigrating to an area where no one else knows their language. When you reflect upon it, Yiey Koum did not have many opportunities in adulthood to continue reading and writing. Married at 16 to someone she did not know, she would give birth to 13 children and have other, more pressing things to do.

When the Khmer Rouge came, she says, they tried to shoot all the people in the village. Fearing for their lives, Yiey Koum and her husband ran away with the children and hid in the woods near the river. A month later, the Khmer Rouge, who seem to have been coming and going through the village at frequent but unpredictable intervals, took away their cows, their pigs, their buffaloes. She was forced to move to a camp where she spent three years building roads, digging the ground, carrying soil. This, she says, gave her a bad back, a problem she complained of at the very beginning of the interview. She adds that the Khmer Rouge had plans to build a big lake. We haven't heard about this particular project, but we know that the Khmer Rouge undertook irrigation projects designed to increase rice production. In their determination to get rid of the educated middle class, the Khmer Rouge had exterminated most of the people with appropriate design and engineering skills. Consequently, those put in charge were often not up to the task. Predictably, such undertakings tended to fail. As for the labourers, they were seen as a dispensable commodity and, according to Yiey Koum, many of them were killed.

She seems to be jumping around in time, so we ask her to recap, hoping that the second telling will restore the correct chronological order. It does not, although it yields some further details. We don't catch the names of the places she refers to, but we learn that she was separated from her husband and children and lived in a house with ten other people. Meanwhile her husband was made to plant tobacco and to carry water over long distances.

It was an incredibly hard life, implying a level of activity and a determination to survive difficult to reconcile with the listless elderly person in front of me. But then, bereavement is a disabling experience and Yiey Koum is still in the early stages of mourning. She may be more like her old self when we come back in a year's time.

When Yiey Koum and her husband came home after the ousting of the Khmer Rouge, they had nothing to live on, so her husband went off to refugee camps to get rice, whilst the rest of the family stayed in Chomnaom. The couple would eventually lead an ordinary life – to the extent that it is possible to have an ordinary life after enduring what they had endured – but, with just three hectares to cultivate, they must have had to make many adjustments.

Yiey Koum is now 71. She has suffered the loss of six children. Her husband, who was five years older than her, died of a heart attack three months ago. Of the seven children left, four have moved away. One works in Thailand as a construction worker, the other main source of employment for Cambodians in Thailand beside plastic factories. One is in Phnom Penh. The other two live in Poipet, a town very close to the Thai border. They send her some money, particularly the one working in Thailand, whose four-year-old daughter lives with her. The other children are all nearby. Another of her sons, whom she describes as suffering from a nervous illness, actually lives with her. The daughter who came to join us lives next door. The last son or daughter lives opposite. She is far from being completely on her own, she has some company, people doing their best to support her and look after her. But this does not make up for her loss.

OM RIM AND TA JOK

—

Chomnaom, February 2015

You can't fail to notice Om Rim and Ta Jok's house. Painted bright blue, it stands new and resplendent on the left-hand side of the dirt road leading to Chomnaom church. The pattern is traditional, with a raised first floor above an open area. Looking at it from a distance, I assume that they have also used traditional materials, but as we get closer, even my untrained eye can see that this is not the case. The house has a timber frame, but the foundations are made of concrete, and the walls and roof consist of galvanised iron sheets. It strikes me as likely to be noisy when it rains, and hot when the sun shines, but it looks solid and watertight and has electricity.

I can see people, quite a few in fact, going up the steps leading to the first floor. They include members of the Catholic community and have come for the blessing of the house by Fr Pedro, whose duties include parish priest of Chomnaom as well as director of the Tep Im Centre. We have been invited to attend the blessing, and have arranged to interview Om Rim and Ta Jok after the ceremony, which celebrates the completion of their

home. There is already quite a crowd assembled upstairs waiting patiently in small groups for Fr Pedro. The pace of life is slow and relaxed here, and people are happy to chat leisurely to one another.

Fr Pedro makes his way to the right-hand corner to join the couple, who will sit on the floor like everyone else, in front of him. He is the one exception: he will not be sitting on the floor, for he has been provided with a low stool in deference to his higher status. The same arrangement is used at Mass. I remember an English priest, who had come with us to Cambodia, telling our little group after celebrating Mass in a floating church on the Tonle Sap from the relative comfort of his special seat, how sorry he had felt for the rest of us. I suppose that our faces and postures had said it all. Besides being a hard surface to be sitting on for any length of time, as wooden boards generally are, the floor had been moving up and down and from side to side. Which is perfectly normal for a church on water, but can make you feel rather queasy if you are not accustomed to spending most of your life on a boat. The floor we are sitting on now is just as hard, but at least it is not rocking.

The blessing ceremony is very much as you might expect, with prayers and the sprinkling of water, followed, when the religious part is over, by the passing round of nibbles: crackers, fruit. Most of those taking part then leave, while we move to the corner with Chanthorn to proceed with the interview. Those who have chosen to remain stay around and continue their conversations, inching gradually closer to listen in, and even put in their two words. Privacy in Chomnaom is not an everyday commodity.

Om Rim and Ta Jok are another example of an arranged marriage. While as far as one can see they fared better than Ming Lin, neither claims to have been blissfully happy. To my question: "What has been the happiest time of your life?" Om Rim replies that she has never been happy because her whole life has been spent working. He answers that he was happier before getting married because he was freer. I suspect what he means is that he had fewer burdens and responsibilities. If not, it must surely have been a factor. They admit all this openly in front of each other and one can only admire their honesty. Unless, that is, they do not expect marriage to bring people happiness. After all, being happy together is something that has appeared relatively late on the scene in the West, even if it is now viewed as essential. Maybe marriage here has more to do, or at least used to have more to do, with following tradition, and with the hope that marriage will bring you children able to support you in your old age.

They are being frank, telling it as it is. Why pussyfoot around? Happiness is a pipedream when you consider what they have lived through. What chance have they had to be happy, when between them they have encountered some of the most appalling tragedies that can befall a human being?

Their stories, although not identical, have much in common. Both were married before, both had a child from this first marriage, and in both cases the child died. Ta Jok's wife died half an hour after giving birth. The baby died one day later. Om Rim's husband ran away to Thailand. She was pregnant, her mother was old, and her sister was ill, so she decided to stay behind rather than go with him. The child died at the age of three. Om Rim and Ta Jok's union was forced on them by the Khmer Rouge because he was a widower. Did they want to marry? *He* didn't care one way or the other, but *she* cared. She did not want to marry him and refused him twice, at which point she was threatened to be separated from her mother if she refused again. Like Ming Lin, she gave in. He was 30, she was 22.

They were not particularly well matched. While both of them came from large rice farming families of respectively 15 and 12 children, and were both half way down the age scale, the similarities stopped there. Her family were Buddhist, his were Catholic. He was a local man born near the river in Chomnaom, whereas until the age of 17, she lived in a province that she describes as "far away", beyond the Tonle Sap, beyond Phnom Penh even. Not being an expert in Cambodian toponymy or, for that matter, knowledgeable about the place-names of any country, I will have to look up where it is later on, on the Internet.

I find out that it is indeed far away, as far away as you can get really, in the South East, quite close to Vietnam. I make a note to ask her more about the move: what happened, how long it took to reach their destination, and – as this too is a place I do not know – the location of the town or village they settled in. She has mentioned going from there to Chomnaom, so it is not Chomnaom. Maybe her husband can show me on a map. I know she can't, since she has said that she is not good at reading.

This is another major difference between Om Rim and Ta Jok, a gender-related difference, in all probability, that has been slow to disappear. As a child, she worked in the fields and didn't go to school whereas he did. In fact, he studied for five years, first in Chomnaom primary school, and then with the Sisters of Providence in Battambang. Not only that, but before going to school, he did not do anything. He was the only boy and his parents didn't want him to work in the rice fields. It was all right for his sisters, though, at least the older ones, and he himself would be forced to eventually, both under the Khmer Rouge and afterwards.

Om Rim and Ta Jok have had two sons together, both now married with children. The older one went to work in Thailand for a while, but is now a farmer in Chomnaom. The younger one works in a Thai factory and regularly sends money to his parents, who have been looking after two of the couple's children for the last five years. These are not the only grandchildren Om Rim and Ta Jok have had staying with them. Indeed, over the years, all bar one have come to live with them at some point or other. I ask Om Rim whether she has found bringing up her grandchildren difficult. I am not surprised at her "Yes", but the reason she gives is something I had overlooked. It was particularly hard, she says, when they were small and were sick at night, because she had to go and pick them up in the dark. They did not have electricity in those days.

Ta Jok's back is all bent and twisted and he no longer farms. He rents out the two hectares of land he still owns. He also gets a little money from cleaning houses. Like most of their neighbours, he and his wife get by as best they can.

OM NY

———

Chomnaom, February 2015

When, knowing that I wished to talk to Buddhists as well as Catholics, Fr Pedro suggested interviewing Om Ny, I objected that she was too young. Om Ny goes to the pagoda, not to Chomnaom Church, so our paths had not crossed very often, but I had spoken to her once or twice. She was usually at home when the pick-up truck bringing us to Chomnaom for the weekend stopped by her house to drop off her daughter, Kimlon, who was studying at the Tep Im Centre. Some of the students who had come to run activities for the local kids, but were not from Chomnaom and needed putting up, would jump off with Kimlon and stay at her house. I had no doubt from the way Om Ny had come up to the truck to say hello that we would get on, but she was significantly younger than the other people we were interviewing, and what we were looking for, at that point, were Cambodians who had been left in charge of grandchildren. Fr Pedro assured me that Om Ny had experience of raising a grandchild. There is no fixed age for becoming a grandmother and, although still in her early 50's, Om Ny had been looking after a granddaughter, whose parents worked in Thailand, since the little girl was weaned.

The greetings over, Om Ny suggests we settle in the area beneath the house, where the air is cooler. This is the place where people come to have a rest or talk during the day. Like Om Rim and Ta Jok's, the house is new and replaces a dwelling built on the same spot. It was already under construction when we came last year, and Kimlon invited us to take a look around. We will be given a proper guided tour of the finished property later on, after the interview. For the moment, we sit and chat. The atmosphere is relaxed, without any of the strain and awkwardness you might expect in a conversation in which one of the parties probes into the life of someone they hardly know. Om Ny wants us to feel welcome and certainly succeeds. From the start, she appears to be happier, more at peace, more optimistic in outlook than the others.

This may be in part a question of personality, although her age is likely to have something to do with it. For a start, she enjoys better health and has more energy. While she mentions at the end that she has been suffering from stomach ache for years, this does not seem to trouble her unduly. It is certainly not in the same league as a life threatening, crippling, or debilitating ailment. Crucially, being younger, she was at a different stage in life during the Khmer Rouge years. It must have been a horrendous experience for someone who had just reached adolescence to be forcibly removed from her normal life and surroundings and turned into a slave because of the twisted thinking and mad ambitions of a paranoid political movement rife with insane schemes. The upheaval compromised her future and she cannot have escaped witnessing some horrific scenes. But, as a single person without descendants, she was spared finding herself powerless to care for, and protect, those she had brought into the world. Unlike the others, her entire adult life still lay ahead. It was not hacked into, forever scarred and wrecked, or, as in Ming Lin's case, mangled, before it had even properly begun. In addition – and this is rare – she came through that brutal period without losing any member of her close family, so the heinous crimes perpetrated by the Khmer Rouge have not left her with the same legacy of hurts.

Om Ny is not from Chomnaom. She is what my grandmother, who came from Normandy and had been a lace maker, called a *"pièce rapportée"*, an expression that she affectionately applied to Michael when we went to visit her, never failing to remind him jokingly about William the Conqueror. That is to say, Om Ny, like Michael, has been added on to the family, like a patch, a piece you insert to repair or embellish a garment. She is an in-law, albeit one who does not come from far, since she was born and grew up in Rohat Tuok, a village approximately seven kilometres North East of Chomnaom. She explains that her parents were rice farmers and that she was number four in a family of six children. When I ask whether she went to school, she replies that she did for a year, when she was about 12, but that she can barely read and write. She would have continued with her studies, except that on arriving in Rohat Tuok the Khmer Rouge rounded up all the young people and sent them to work in the fields. And with that, her schooling came to an end.

It is hard to believe that the leadership of the Khmer Rouge, themselves beneficiaries of scholarships that took them to French universities and enabled them to be educated to a high standard, should have been prepared to confine people to near illiteracy in this way. Admittedly, stopping people from learning to read and write pales into insignificance when compared to the horrific acts of outrageous cruelty the Khmer Rouge proved themselves capable of, yet the mind boggles.

I too went to university in Paris, albeit later than the Khmer Rouge leaders. I am familiar with what student life was like, with the conflicting ideologies one encountered, the many debates taking place, the various political and intellectual undercurrents liable to erupt at any moment into demonstrations and counterdemonstrations as happened in May 1968. But beyond the differences of opinion found in all societies, although possibly not always as visibly as in France, there was a general consensus around certain basic moral values. I have struggled with the question of how people who had been exposed to such values could, in the late 20th century, not simply commit, but actually instigate and endorse the appalling atrocities that the Khmer Rouge inflicted on the Cambodian people (and any other person unfortunate enough to find themselves in Cambodia at that time).

I recently came across a book by William Shawcross entitled *Sideshow* that contains a number of pointers, the germ of an answer. It investigates the involvement of the United States in the spreading of the Vietnam conflict into Cambodia, an arena viewed as less important than Vietnam, some sort of collateral damage, or minor show. One of the chapters in the book examines the origins of Cambodian communism, including the intellectual journey of the main leaders of the Khmer Rouge. What particularly held my interest was the author's summary of the thesis written by Khieu Sampham, who was to become Head of State from 1976 until 1979 and who received a life sentence for crimes against humanity in 2014, before being found guilty of genocide in 2018.

Rather chillingly, Khieu Samphan's thesis, which was completed in 1959, made a series of points that either remain valid today, or else have parallels in contemporary Cambodian society. These include the essentially agricultural nature of the Cambodian economy, the small size of plots, the reliance of Khmer farmers on moneylenders charging extortionate rates, the importing of goods catering for the needs and tastes of the wealthier members of society and/or detrimental to domestic industrial expansion and the local economy, the exploitative nature of certain types of aid, the concentration of work opportunities in unproductive service jobs or in the civil service. The core of the thesis – in many ways its most noteworthy aspect given what happened later – revolved round the argument that industry could only be developed following the development of agriculture, which, in turn, required people to be moved out of towns into agricultural work, organised into cooperatives, and, at a later stage, transferred into industrial jobs. However, as Shawcross emphasizes, Khieu Samphan favoured persuasion through political education, not the imposition of changes by force. He argued that understanding and patience would be needed to ensure that the changes received general support among the population. As we know, implementation would turn out quite differently, and compulsion would become one of the hall marks of the Khmer Rouge takeover. However, the overall rationale is interesting and sheds some light on events that appear beyond our comprehension.

Om Ny's family found itself split up. Her mother took care of the younger children, while her father was sent to farm rice in another location. Three years would go by before they were reunited following the arrival of the Vietnamese, which enabled them to return to Rohat Tuok. Were they pleased to see the Vietnamese? She has no hesitation: "Yes, Pol Pot killed people." (As with the others, for "Pol Pot" read "the Khmer Rouge".)

In 1982, the father of Om Ny's future husband came to ask her parents for her hand. The two older couples knew one another but, according to Om Ny, the young people had never seen each other. Disconcertingly, when we talk to her husband the following year, he remembers the past differently. He believes that they first met when he was visiting relatives who lived in Rohat Tuok. If he is right, she clearly made rather more of an impression on him than he did on her.

In the event, Om Ny went along with her parents' wishes and, thankfully, fell in love with her husband-to-be when she saw him at the Kulten festival. When we ask what the Kulten festival is, she just repeats the word *Kulten*, echoed by our interpreter. It is clear from their reaction that we are talking about an obviously important social gathering – a kind of boat race, it seems – but, contrary to their manifest expectations, we have never heard of it.

I look *Kulten* up when we get back to England, a process hampered by the fact that we have misheard what Om Ny said. Not only is the festival not called *Kulten* but *Kathen*, but outside Cambodia it goes by the name of *Kathina*. Kathen, or Kathina, is a traditional celebration observed by Theravada Buddhists, who form about 95% of the Khmer population. It lasts just over a day and is held in every pagoda across the country. Given that there are today over 3000 pagodas in Cambodia, we are talking of quite a lot of activity. The exact date varies from pagoda to pagoda, but must be set within a 29 day window based on the Buddhist lunar calendar. This window generally corresponds to the period from mid-October to mid-November in the Gregorian calendar.

Kathen is a joyful religious ceremony that marks the end of the monks' confinement to the temple compound during the rainy season. Its most distinctive feature is an ancient ritual that involves offering new robes to the monks paid for by the laity. It is also a general alms-giving/fund-raising event that brings in other types of donations, for instance money to repair and maintain the pagoda, or to help build schools and hospitals. And it does include boat races.

The wedding took place in the bride's village the day after the Kathen festival. A week later, the newly weds moved to Chomnaom, where they lived with his parents, whom Om Ny would take care of for the rest of their lives.

Om Ny and her husband have had six children: three boys and three girls, who are now between 20 and 32. The three boys are all married and work in a plastics factory in Bangkok. They regularly send money, although not as much as when they were single. The oldest son has twins who are both in Chomnaom. One of them (the little girl mentioned above) is looked after by Om Ny, the other by the maternal grandmother. The parents visit once a year. Om Ny's other sons have both recently become fathers, but the children, who are still babies, are in Thailand. The oldest of the three girls is married with one child and lives next door. The next one is Kimlon, who is studying in Battambang, and the youngest is at the Don Bosco training centre in Sihanoukville.

The house, says Om Ny as she takes us round, cost 210,000 bahts, around 7000 dollars. People, here, tend to discuss building costs in Thai bahts, possibly because most of the money is likely to have come one way or another from work done in Thailand. The money for the build reportedly came from their savings, but the children might be regarded as having contributed indirectly through the funds they have sent over the years.

There is a large and pleasant garden filled with a variety of tropical plants: mangoes, papayas, oranges, sugar cane. There is also a pond at the back, currently only half full as it is the dry season. The water, Om Ny informs us, is not clean enough for cooking and is used for watering the plants. Drinking water comes from rain water, collected from the roof into large stone jars before it is transferred into more manageable containers. The kitchen is not located in the house but in a small building next to it. It is devoid of the kind of equipment found in a Western home, but, on the other hand, boasts an impressive assortment of knives, including the kind of cleavers necessary for boning and carving meat, in addition to a range of pots and pans. It is all very tidy. All the utensils are lined up along the walls leaving an open space in the middle. Cooking is done outside in a pot set over a wood fire. To the left of the kitchen is another separate building with a squat down toilet.

Apart from being more solid and spacious than the previous building, the new house offers the great advantage of being connected to the grid. Having electricity has had a big impact on Om Ny's life. They use electricity for lighting, for the television, and also for running the pond water pump. Their bill comes to $10 a month. Life is not trouble free. Om Ny is concerned that her daughters need to get jobs, but she is positive. Hers is a close-knit family willing to help each other. She is right. As it happens, Kimlon, who has nearly finished her accountancy degree, confided to us recently that she does not want to go and live away, as she sees it as her responsibility to provide money to support her younger sister. I suppose, she thinks it will be easier for her to save money if she stays nearby. We'll see what the future brings.

Despite the uncertainties hanging over Chomnaom, the lack of opportunities, the poor conditions, Om Ny rejoices in the knowledge that her children are prospering and have enough money. It is a heart warming story after all we have heard, a story which shows that, despite the bad press that they sometimes receive, sponsorships – and foreign aid more generally – can help improve living standards and people's prospects. What would Om Ny describe as the happiest period of her life? With relief I hear her say: "This time."

KROO YAT

Chomnaom, February 2015

As the leader of the Catholic community, Kroo Yat is a familiar figure to us, but our meetings have always had an official, formal quality. He is not someone we have ever chatted to. We have not been to his house, and we have yet to meet his wife. He is mainly known to us as the person in charge of making announcements at the end of Mass, when he comes to the front to read out the proceeds of the last collection, to report on the parish's finances, or to announce forthcoming events. And, if there are visitors, to express the community's appreciation of their presence in Chomnaom.

Michael and I normally sit down among the congregation rather than on the chairs set out on the side for those who find it difficult to sit on the floor. Unless, that is, we have already attended a church service on that day, at which point our bodies unashamedly proclaim that enough is enough. True, the floor is not wonderfully comfortable, but sitting at the same level as other people helps us feel more involved, less obviously outsiders (or, perhaps, less obviously old). The problem is that Khmer

Masses tend to last quite a long time. Khmer is less concise a language than English and uses significantly more words to express a particular idea. The ritual therefore takes longer. The "Our Father", for instance, uses twice as many words as in English. So it takes twice as long.

By the time Kroo Yat approaches the lectern, we are getting stiff and achy and, dare I say, rather looking forward to the time when we will at last be able to stand up and stretch our legs. We have got up to go to communion, but, however skilful you are at picking a moment that maximises the time you spend standing, waiting until a substantial queue has formed and then making your way purposefully to the end, hoping against hope that no one in the line will smilingly motion to you to come and stand in front of them in the queue, the respite always proves far too short.

Over the years we have been going to Chomnoam, we have learnt that when Kroo Yat makes his way to the lectern, the end is not yet in sight, and relief will be a little while yet. Especially if we have just arrived, or it is our last visit. Kroo Yat takes his responsibilities seriously, and wants to make certain we know that people are pleased and grateful that we are here. A couple of sentences will not do. Add to this that, as he is addressing English speakers but speaking in Khmer on behalf of Khmer parishioners, his speech has to be interpreted for our benefit. We are then invited to come to the front and say a few words.

Great, you might think, another opportunity to stand up. Except that, on this occasion, the rest of the congregation stay put, and standing up entails rising on the spot with all eyes turned towards you. Quite a challenge, believe me, after over an hour on the floor. Any hope we might have entertained of performing this demanding feat in a manner that looks remotely effortless and graceful soon evaporates, as we concentrate on the more important task of keeping our balance and avoiding falling on any of our immediate neighbours. Having reached the front, we bravely launch into Khmer, only to return after a couple of sentences to the safer shores of a language we can actually speak. Once again Fr Pedro will usually act as interpreter, unless, as happened once, he gets confused – understandably, as he speaks four languages – and translates *our* English into *his* English. But people are listening attentively and will put him right if need be. Then comes going back to our places and the chance to practise sitting down in one fluid movement. As we begin our descent, the tiny spaces we were supposed to fit in grow and grow under the dual influence of kindness towards us and self-protection, leaving us to ponder briefly on the foolishness of sitting on the floor. I guess that one day, when we are really, really, really old, we will become humbler, or wiser, or both, and give in.

Fortunately, Kroo Yat's interview does not take place sitting on the floor of the church, which, I am sure, would present far fewer difficulties to him than to us, but sitting around a rectangular table in Chomnaom presbytery. And Kroo Yat, whom I have always found slightly intimidating – he is referred to as *Kroo*, which means 'teacher', and conducts himself as someone used to having a certain authority – proves very open and friendly.

The origins he mentions are unexceptional. Now 66, he was born in Chomnaom from parents who were rice farmers. Unlike most of the other interviewees, however, he went to the local primary school, as did his youngest brother, though not the rest of his siblings. He was the eldest child and, from the time he was weaned, lived next door to his parents with his grandmother. She was the one who supported his education, which lasted until he was 12, when poverty stopped him from carrying on with his studies.

Whether because he felt inclined to, because his level of education was superior to that of other Catholics, or just because the opportunity presented itself, I do not know, but at the age of 15, Kroo Yat started working with the Church. Among other things, he helped his grandmother in her work as cook for the parish priest, Fr Jean Badré, which brought him into contact with the local bishop, Mgr Paul Tep Im.

He recounts how the take over by the Khmer Rouge was followed by an announcement on the radio that all foreigners should leave for their own country. He explains how Mgr Tep Im went from Battambang to Chomnaom, and then left for Sway Sisophon in the company of Fr Jean Badré with the intention of going to Thailand. As we know, both were killed on the way.

Meanwhile, Kroo Yat and five other Catholic families were moved a few kilometres from Chomnaom to a location that we do not catch. Kroo Yat was made to work in the rice field during the day and, unusually, and rather surprisingly, was asked to teach in the evening. He presses on with his life story without specifying what he taught, and when, back home, I come to write up his account, I make a note to ask for further details at our next visit. Having set out his duties, Kroo Yat goes on to describe how everyone ate together and how there was no religious freedom. As it would have been risky to meet with the other Catholics to pray, he prayed alone, in secret. Otherwise, he seems to have been left in relative peace.

Following the arrival of the Vietnamese, he first went to a refugee camp, and then returned to Chomnaom. There was no priest in Chomnaom, so he would go to the camp to attend Mass and bring back communion hosts for the members of the Catholic community who had come back to Chomnaom. He taught Khmer to local children and would have carried on doing so, but the Vietnamese became suspicious when they heard that he was Catholic and he was told to stop, although he was allowed to teach for the Church.

After the Vietnamese's departure, Kroo Yat was employed by the Ministry of Health to compile lists of babies and vaccination lists, and to give hygiene classes. As the salary he had been promised showed no sign of materialising, he continued his rice farming activities. In 1980, unable to go to France to study for the priesthood, he married a young Buddhist whom he had met at the refugee camp. He did not marry in church, presumably because there was no priest around to preside over the marriage. The religious ceremony would come much later, in 2008 or 2009.

He and his wife have had seven children, four sons and three daughters. He lists them in age order, one by one, in a manner that recalls the systematic, methodical way with which he approaches the making of Church announcements. He tells us where they live, whether they are married, whether they have children. It is a lot to take in and we get lost, but we gather that the youngest child is 17 and is still studying in Battambang, and that some of the others work in Thailand. Those in Thailand send money and come back from time to time, but it is Kroo Yat and his wife who bring up their children. The rest of the sons and daughters are mostly in Chomnaom, and would seem to be living with him. It amounts to quite a lot of people for one household, so I ask him how many they are. Amazingly, he is not quite sure! Around 19, he thinks. He is still doing some work for the Church and a little rice farming. He used to own five hectares, but he has given four of them to his children and finds life difficult. Who would not in a household of 20 or so?

The happiest time in his life? It will be no surprise to hear that he was happiest before Pol Pot, when he was single, independent, unencumbered by all the responsibilities he now has to shoulder.

Being a pillar of the Catholic community, Kroo Yat has an in-depth first-hand knowledge of life in Chomnaom, so we seize the opportunity to ask him what he considers to be the main issue for local people. This year, he replies, the problem for people is that the harvest has been poor and many farmers have incurred big debts. The fact is that it is hard to make a living out of rice farming. First, because without an irrigation system, you can only produce one crop per year. Secondly, unless you are relatively well off, you cannot hold on to your crop. You have to sell it straightaway in order to repay the loans you have taken out to cover essential expenses like purchasing rice seed and fertilizer or hiring labour. So, you sell when everyone else is also selling. Even if you were able to wait, you would have nowhere to store your rice. The result is that crops are bought up by big companies when rice is plentiful and prices are low, stored in huge barns, and sold on when the temporary glut vanishes and prices rise.

It is all depressingly reminiscent of the social injustices and exploitative practices denounced by the prophet Amos nearly 3000 years ago:

> Listen to this, you who trample on the needy
> and try to suppress the poor people of the country,
> you who say, "When will New Moon be over
> so that we can sell our corn,
> and sabbath, so that we can market our wheat?
> Then by lowering the bushel, raising the shekel,
> by swindling and tampering with the scales,
> we can buy up the poor for money,
> and the needy for a pair of sandals,
> and get a price even for the sweepings of the wheat."
> (*Amos 8: 4-7, The Jerusalem Bible*)

Before winding up, we ask Kroo Yat for his view of how life in Chomnaom has changed over the last ten years. Again, his reply focuses on rice growing. Rice used to be cultivated using traditional farming practices, he says, tilling the land with ox-drawn ploughs. But animals have been replaced by machinery. Those used in Chomnaom are of a fairly basic type: simple two-wheel hand tractors (*kojuns*) that still require a degree of manual labour, four wheel tractors where people are more affluent, that require fewer people. Planting in Chomnaom is still done by hand, as is harvesting, but combine harvesters are increasingly being introduced and are a potential threat to employment opportunities. "Could new crops or other means of earning a living be introduced?" "You need to have studied to undertake new things", he answers, "and most of the current population is illiterate." Kroo Yat's prospects may be better than most, but the picture he paints is a matter for concern.

WRITING IT UP

England, 2015-2016

As I write up the interviews, I come across a number of issues: inconsistencies, missing information and discontinuities, points that need to be clarified or developed. Some problems only appear when I try to turn the notes into narratives and notice that certain things don't add up. Others, such as Om Ren's baffling story about her husband having to build an oven, are not new. They surfaced during the conversation, but I chose to let them pass and move on in order to maintain momentum.

Inevitably, some stories require more work than others. Om Borei's account is clear and comprehensive and writing it up is straightforward. I discover with relief that the most distressing aspects of Ming Lin's narrative leave no room for confusion and won't need revisiting. A number of stories, however, prove to have significant gaps or contradictory statements. The gaps will have to be filled in, the contradictions resolved. And, in almost all cases, precise dates and locations have yet to be established.

As, during the year, I think of our next trip, I can't completely banish from my mind that some of the people who have so kindly allowed me to peer into their lives may have passed away by the time we next get there. As it turns out, what awaits us is something else, more uncommon, unforeseeable in fact, and although less final than death, it will leave me quite despondent for a while.

The next section deals with the interviews that took place during that trip (2016). These interviews were not an exact replica of the first round. Not only did a number of constraints prevent us from adopting the same schedule, but the format had to be flexible and take into account what had been said the year before. I approached certain conversations with a bespoke agenda in mind, but others were more free wheeling. It all depended on how many issues the writing up had thrown up, and the number of opportunities that arose, in the course of the meetings, for elaborating on what people had shared in 2015, or for branching off into new areas.

In broad terms, the interactions tended to revolve around two very different topics: life under the Khmer Rouge, and changes in the interviewees' circumstances, if any. These recurrent themes provide the main structure, with an initial subdivision by location, and then, within each chapter, by individual contributions. There then follows another glimpse into our visits.

PART THREE

2016

LIFE UNDER THE KHMER ROUGE: BATTAMBANG INTERVIEWS

Battambang, 2016

OM REN

High on the list of issues to be resolved concerning our hosts' life during the Khmer Rouge era is how Om Ren's husband came to be ordered to build an oven, within a fortnight, under pain of death, despite his lack of relevant expertise. We are conscious that this odd demand may just have been one more item in the catalogue of irrational, arbitrary decisions taken by the Khmer Rouge. Nevertheless, we both find it puzzling and wonder how it came about. When we probe further during our 2016 visit, the beginning of an explanation starts to emerge. Not the whole story, but at least a set of possible embryonic scenarios.

Expanding on what she said last year, Om Ren tells us that her husband had been a Lon Nol soldier, and that he had received an injury that he endeavoured to hide. Whether the Khmer Rouge discovered this injury, or found out about his past career, perhaps following a denunciation, she does not specify, but there can be no doubt that his hitherto hidden past would have provided the Khmer Rouge with a sufficient reason to threaten, or just kill him.

Why they chose to ask him to build an oven rather than simply execute him without more ado may be due to a number of reasons. Maybe the policy had changed, or maybe this particular group happened to be less cruel and blood thirsty than some of the others. It is reported that there were variations between the regions in the degree of alacrity with which directives from the centre were applied. This may have been one of the more lenient groups. Alternatively, Om Ren's husband may have proved to be such a valuable group leader that the Khmer Rouge decided to offer him a conditional reprieve, a chance to redeem himself by building something they needed. Or else he may have denied that he had ever been in Lon Nol's army, claiming that all the while he had been working as a builder, and those in charge were trying to verify his story by testing his building expertise. That the nature of the task lay outside his normal line of work is unlikely to have mattered to them. In fact, they may have deliberately chosen to set him a difficult challenge.

As we know, Om Ren's husband completed the assignment in time and in so doing escaped death. However, his unfortunate spell in Lon Nol's army would come to haunt him again after the Vietnamese invasion, when the fear that he might be arrested for his military career prompted them to move to a refugee camp on the Thai border.

OM RI

Another story I am keen to hear more about is the birth of Om Ri's son. I am intrigued by the person who only had a walk-on part in Om Ri's account of her prolonged labour, but whose intervention seems to have been a crucial factor in its successful outcome. Who was this person? What led her to come to a pregnant woman's assistance and were there any repercussions for her?

Om Ri replies that the doctor was a widow, whose husband, also a doctor, had been killed by the Khmer Rouge because of his profession. Forced to move from Phnom Penh, she owed her survival to the fact that the Khmer Rouge was unaware that she, too, was medically qualified. She came forward following an appeal by the authorities for someone who knew how to deliver babies and, according to Om Ri, did not suffer any adverse consequences. This too may be accounted for by some softening of attitudes, some rethinking. Or perhaps the Khmer Rouge took the view that many women have experience of attending to women in labour and did not bother to pursue the matter. Whatever the case, that doctor's willingness to put her own life at stake for someone else's sake remains admirable, a bright spot among the myriad instances of inhumanity.

OM PRANYA

I have several questions about people's movements. They mostly involve the inhabitants of Chomnaom, but I take advantage of our visit to Om Pranya to get a clearer picture of the evacuation of Battambang. When I ask when the city was emptied, Om Pranya replies that she is not sure, but she thinks it was around ten days after Mgr Tep Im's last Mass. This tallies with François Ponchaud's account in *The Cathedral of the Rice Paddy*, which, on page 149, gives Sunday 13 April as the date of Mgr Tep Im's last Mass, 17 April as the date the Khmer Rouge occupied Battambang (which might mean that the soldiers she saw from inside the church were an advance party), and 24 April as the day when the inhabitants were driven out.

She describes how the Khmer Rouge told everybody to get out of Battambang, because, they said, they wanted to make improvements. It would take three days – or so the Khmer

Rouge claimed – after which people would be able to return to their homes. No instructions were given about where they should go. Everyone left together taking with them a few things for what they thought would be a three-day absence.

Where did they stay? Some people stayed with friends, others in pagodas. Some slept in fields, or on the road, until the Khmer Rouge organised them.

When we move on to the personal losses Om Pranya suffered at that time, she tells us that, according to her older brother's sister-in-law, her brother and his whole family were taken by truck to a high mountain near Sihanoukville, where they were thrown down a waterfall. There were many such executions during the Pol Pot period. Indeed, Om Pranya had a nephew who is thought to have died in a similar way at Wat Samrong Knong, one of several killing sites near Battambang.

Of all these macabre places, the one that made the deepest impression on me is Phnom Sampeov. Phnom Sampeov is occasionally referred to as the Sampeov mountain, probably on account of its steep sides, which contrast with the flatness of the plain around. It is, actually, more of a hill than a mountain – the Khmer term *Phnom* can refer to both. Less well known and attracting far fewer tourists than the Killing Fields of Choeung Ek, the notorious extermination camp near Phnom Penh, Phnom Sampeov is just as gruesome and chilling, but more stark, with no crowds and few trappings of tourism. There are no audio guides. There is only you, a few others, and the memory of what happened here.

We have been to Phnom Sampeov a couple of times. Ten thousand people are thought to have died in this tranquil spot. If you want to, you can climb up to the top of the hill and stand where people were thrown down a gully. Lower down, a flight of steps leads to the end of the gully and an underground chamber with a display of some of the victims' skulls. A place where life

pauses out of respect for these extinguished lives. A cave filled with the hush of the living and the dead, where speech stops and movement slows. Sharing in the sombre mood, the living, stunned and sorrowful, stand, sit down, or kneel, to pay homage to the dead.

And then the fortunate you that you are climbs back up into the fresh air.

Unlike Om Pranya's older brother, the nephew whom she believes to have been killed at Wat Samrong Knong did not belong to the military. He was a teacher and found himself caught up in one of the purges aimed at eradicating educated people. From what she will tell us the following year, his death took place in 1977, at the hands of what she puzzlingly refers to as *Pol Pot ti pi* (the second Pol Pot). She goes on to explain that there were two waves of Khmer Rouge soldiers. The first group (*Pol Pot ti muy*) was made up of people from the North West and had some compassion. The second group originated from the South West; they did not speak Khmer well and were more ruthless.

When, in 2015, I questioned Om Pranya about the length of the Khmer Rouge regime, her reply came instantaneously: 3 years, 8 months, 20 days. The speed of her response and the precision of the information surprised me. I ask her about that. "Oh", she says, "everyone knows that."

LIFE UNDER THE KHMER ROUGE: CHOMNAOM INTERVIEWS

Chomnaom, 2016

OM RIM & TA JOK

In all the Chomnaom interviews, we spend some time going over people's movements during the Khmer Rouge period. Our first port of call is Om Rim and Ta Jok's house. To make up for our poor knowledge of Cambodian place names and geography, we arrive armed with a map which we spread out on the floor between us. Smiling and looking at ease, Om Rim confirms that, as we thought, the place where she was born is called Svay Rieng. Soon everyone is poring over the map to pinpoint Svay Rieng. It takes an enormous amount of time and a lot of talking and scrutinising, with fingers moving up, down, and across the map. There is not much call for map-reading skills around here. Even Chanthorn is having difficulty locating places. We eventually spot Svay Rieng, almost as far as you can go in the South East of Cambodia without finding yourself in Vietnam. Om Rim explains that her father heard that land was cheaper in the North West. How did he hear this, I wonder, when he was living miles and miles away. Could it have been by word of mouth, at such a distance? Or was it reported on the radio, perhaps with the aim to attract people? Anyway, he decided to sell his property and move. And that was that.

Even now, to uproot your family and relocate so far away would not be trivial, but in those days it must have been extremely daunting. They travelled by taxi, almost certainly not the kind of taxi you have in mind, but a pick-up truck open at the back. You come across a lot of these trucks in Cambodia, where they remain a very popular form of transport for carrying not only goods, but people too. Travelling in the open air without any form of restraint or protection is something the police would not look too kindly on in the West, but is commonplace over there. Unsurprisingly, the trip took two days, with a night in Phnom Penh. "It was very difficult", she says.

They settled in a village called Nimitt, 20 kilometres from Poipet, a town on the Thailand-Cambodia border, a main crossing point between the two countries. They had quite literally moved from one end of the country to the other.

They lived in Nimitt until the arrival of the Khmer Rouge, when they were made to move to a location some 12 kilometres from Chomnaom, where Ta Jok, who had been assigned to plough rice fields, was the leader of the girls' rice planting team. Om Rim reiterates that, had she persisted in refusing to marry Ta Jok, she would have been separated from her mother, adding that there was another reason why she did not want to remarry: she knew that her husband was still alive. What would have happened to Ta Jok, if he had refused to marry her, I ask. "It wouldn't have been a problem", he replies.

To build on what Ming Lin told us about the way the Khmer Rouge conducted wedding ceremonies, I ask Om Rim and Ta Jok to recount what happened. They tell us that they were married in a big meeting hall built with materials taken from the houses around. The celebration took place at night and involved twenty-five couples. They demonstrate how they had to raise their hands in the air together to mark their agreement, a symbolic gesture that they had to do simultaneously with all the other couples. After getting married, they were given their own house. They still have the house and one of his sisters lives there.

As for Om Rim's former husband, in a development not unlike what happened to Om Borei, he came back to Cambodia in 1980, shortly after the official fall of the Pol Pot regime, and asked her to come and live with him again as a couple. She refused. He is now a monk in Bangkok.

YIEY KOUM

In an attempt to clarify what happened to Yiey Koum during that period, I ask her to take us again through her story. As far as we can reconstruct the sequence of events, the family initially fled from Chomnaom to try and escape the Khmer Rouge, but were then forcibly taken to a Khmer Rouge camp at Ou Chuob, nine kilometres to the East. Yiey Koum is convinced that she would have been killed had she not gone to Ou Chuob, and believes that the reason why there were not more casualties in Chomnaom is that people moved away.

For the next three years the rest of Yiey Koum's family would live in Ou Chuob. As for Yiey Koum, she was sent to work in another place, from which she would come back to Ou Chuob at harvest time. She describes the clothes they wore: black shirts and trousers with white buttons, brown hats, and sandals with cross pieces made from rubber tyres. She explains that, contrary to what I thought, people were not issued with black clothes; what they were given were white clothes, which they were told to boil up with the bark of a local tree in order to dye them black. This, presumably, accounts for the white buttons.

Following the arrival of the Vietnamese, everyone returned to Chomnaom. They would not be there long. Two weeks later the Khmer Rouge were back, so Yiey Koum and her family set off by cart and drove across the rice fields to Mongkol Borei, 25 kilometres to the North East, a place where, three days later, her ten-year-old daughter would be caught in some indiscriminate shooting and die. They did not return home for good until, for the second time, the Vietnamese drove out the Khmer Rouge.

More than any other account, Yiey Koum's narrative conveys the disarray of a people surrounded by guerrilla warfare, tossed about in a sea of contradictory rumours, afraid to be caught in the skirmishes erupting all around, reduced to fleeing away from the sounds of guns in the manner of a flock of birds that veer together first left, then right, then left again, or setting off on their own when threatened by imminent danger. Listening to her, one can imagine the confusion that must have reigned, the people's panic, their desperate attempts to find refuge in a safer place.

OM NY

I can't remember whether the husband of the youngest of our interviewees, Om Ny, was around when we talked to her last year (2015). If he was, he did not take part in the conversation. This time, when we arrive, he is resting in a hammock under the house. As he is not moving, we don't notice him at first. When we do, we invite him to join us and tell us about his life.

He was born in Chomnaom, he says, and is around two years older than Om Ny. Having been brought up in different locations, the couple, who did not marry until 1982, were not affected by the Khmer Rouge rule in identical ways. Thus, he recollects witnessing people being shot when the Khmer Rouge arrived in Chomnaom. He escaped to Sway Sisophon, a town 15 kilometres North of Chomnaom, which, at the time, had not yet been conquered by the Khmer Rouge. The Khmer

Rouge would only reach Sway Sisophon six months later, at which point he was sent back to Chomnaom, before being forced to move to Ou Chuob, the same camp Yiey Koum's family were sent to. He was made to dig canals, along with people from all sorts of places: Phnom Penh, Battambang, Poipet. Everyone was treated the same and worked together, he says, but town dwellers tended to suffer more. Sometimes, people died on the road because they had no food or water. When I ask about the damage done in Chomnaom, he replies that the contents of his house were stolen, but the structure was left intact. This corroborates Yiey Koum's claim that the Khmer Rouge focused their attention on larger houses, probably because dismantling substantial dwellings provided materials with which to erect the sort of communal buildings Om Rim and Ta Jok were married in. With regard to the number of villagers killed, he can only remember three, but believes there were many more.

KROO YAT

When we meet with Kroo Yat, we begin by going back to what happened to him during the Pol Pot period. Where did he go when the Khmer Rouge arrived in Chomnaom? He wasn't there, he says, he had escaped to Mongkol Borei. With his usual gift for providing an overview, he explains that the Khmer Rouge and Lon Nol forces were still at war, that the area between Chomnaom and Rohat Tuok was full of Khmer Rouge, but that Route No 5, further to the North West, was held by Lon Nol. So when the inhabitants of Chomnaom were warned of the impending arrival of the Khmer Rouge, many of them decided to flee before the Khmer Rouge got to Chomnaom.

He himself did not remain long in Mongkol Borei. At Mgr Tep Im's request, he moved to Battambang to teach Khmer and catechism, returning weekly to Mongkol Borei to visit his parents.

Seeking confirmation of what I have been told by others, I ask what happened when the Khmer Rouge arrived. "I don't know", he replies, "I wasn't there." He has indeed just told us so, but I thought he might have heard reports of what took place. I hope he does not think that I was trying to trip him up.

This will only occur to me later, but Kroo Yat's account implies that the Khmer Rouge passed through Chomnaom *before* assuming control of Battambang. In my mind, the Khmer Rouge had begun by gaining control of Battambang and gone on to Chomnaom from there. Replicating – or, more accurately, anticipating – the direction of our own travels. History created in our image.

When Battambang was evacuated, Kroo Yat came back to Chomnaom. As Om Pranya explained, the Khmer Rouge did not issue directives at that stage beyond getting out of the city, so Chomnaom would have been the obvious place for him to go to.

Although Kroo Yat found Chomnaom much the same as before, life was about to undergo a radical transformation with the abolition of private property, a month or so after his arrival. He relates that everything became communal, and that you were required to hand in what you owned, from your saucepans to your fields and cows. There was no option. It was a matter of comply or be killed. Predictably, everyone complied.

He was allocated to one of the youth teams. There were three of these, each numbering one hundred youths. The youth teams did work that required strength, such as building roads and digging trenches. They slept together in schools, moving according to where they were asked to work. Most people were assigned to places that were not too far from their home village, but those whose work was not considered to be up to the mark would be sent further away as a punishment.

I have read that the Khmer Rouge shot intellectuals and that even wearing glasses, a tell-tale sign of education, could be dangerous. I am intrigued that Kroo Yat was not shot. Handling the question in his customary methodical fashion, he embarks on a clear, well-structured analysis: "*ti muy*" (firstly), "*ti pi*" (secondly). His scholarly approach strikes me as highly ironical, given the topic under consideration. His main asset, he says, was that he knew a lot about working in a rice field. He could construct a cart out of wood, for example. He may not have had any actual practical experience, but he knew all there was to know about farming.

At this point, he suddenly turns to address Chanthorn and the two of them engage in a long friendly conversation, which, needless to say, we are unable to follow, but which, from their smiles and the way they bat questions at each other, they appear to find most enjoyable.

After this little interlude, during which, Chanthorn informs us, he was asked by Kroo Yat whether he, Chanthorn, knows how to plough – which he does – we return to the subject under discussion. The Khmer Rouge were perfectly aware that he could read and write, Kroo Yat asserts, so much so that later on they asked him to teach people how to read. He would organise work in the rice field during the day, and at night teach people how to read. In the absence of books, or even chalk, he would write on a board using dry clay. The students would watch and remember. I am tempted to point out that the outcome of his efforts seems to me to be a touch optimistic – if only things were that simple! – but this is not the right moment to discuss the relative merits and drawbacks of particular teaching methods. Having read that the Khmer Rouge were in the habit of burning books and made a great show of it, I confine myself to asking: "What was the purpose of teaching people to read? What was there to read?" He does not know, he only knows that the teacher would think of something – a letter, I suppose, or a word – and draw this on the board for the students to memorize.

Back home, I come across an article on the website of Yale University's Genocide Studies Program that addresses the issue on my mind: what, exactly, was the Khmer Rouge's position on reading and writing? According to George Chigas and Dmitri Mosyakov, the authors of *Literacy and Education under the Khmer Rouge*, although the ability to read and write was widely perceived as grounds for persecution, so much so that people avoided wearing glasses in order no to be targeted, "education per se was not anathema to the regime". What the Khmer Rouge abhorred was the French model of education and what they considered to be its corruptive influence. Farmers with basic literacy skills were not viewed as posing a significant threat, as shown by the fact that the ability to read and write was an essential requirement in the recruitment of Khmer Rouge cadres.

Furthermore, they argue, while initially concentrating their efforts on agricultural development, the Khmer Rouge intended to teach literacy – perhaps they thought the ability to access their propaganda in print form might enhance its reach and effectiveness. Education was to be rolled out in a carefully controlled manner, with an emphasis on technical subjects and on raising the masses' political awareness. Tellingly, what is given pride of place in the Party's four-year plan, drawn up in 1976, is not a teacher's mastery of their subject, but their ability to convey revolutionary consciousness. I doubt this was a criterion that Kroo Yat fulfilled, but there can't have been too many literate people to choose from in Chomnaom.

CHANGES AND DEVELOPMENTS IN 2015: BATTAMBANG

Battambang, 2016

OM BOREI

When we turn to what's happened over the past 12 months, the conversation tends to centre on our hosts' children and grandchildren. Om Borei's own life hasn't changed much, but her daughter and son-in-law have given up the sandal-making business in favour of running an Internet café from the house during the evening. And indeed, when we leave, we notice a group of youths clicking away at a small array of computers set under the porch near the entrance to the house.

OM REN

Last year, Om Ren came to the interview accompanied by three of her grandchildren: two girls whose mother was in Phnom Penh and a little boy whose mother lives with Om Ren. She tells us that they still live with her. Now 10 and 11, the girls attend primary school in a nearby pagoda and are enrolled in

TESOL (English) classes. Their father, who has remarried and whom the younger girl has never met, never sends any money, but Om Ren's daughter, who is studying in Phnom Penh thanks to a sponsorship, makes monthly payments of $50 and visits every three months. There is reference to a possible marriage with someone from Germany prior to the girls joining their mother in the capital.

Om Ren's grandson is now six. He does not go to school and spends all day at home. However, there is a chance that he might be accepted in a centre for children with learning difficulties due to open in the vicinity.

OM PRANYA

When we go and see Om Pranya, we find her with visitors: a daughter who lives in Pailin and her two-year-old child. Sadly, the daughter who was being treated for hepatitis passed away since our last visit. She left a five-year-old girl whose upbringing has now become Om Pranya's responsibility.

OM RI

Om Ri has both good news and bad news. The good news is that she has gained weight. Most people in the West would not regard putting on weight as something to be pleased about, but she does. The weight gain is not exactly what you would describe as striking. She does not look any bigger to me than last year. I would still describe her as emaciated, but I guess it is good news.

We are sitting under the kiosk in the middle of the garden of the Tep Im Centre, Om Ri on a bench, the rest of us (Chanthorn, Michael and I) on plastic chairs. She has folded her legs under her and tucked her feet to the side, a posture which I use in church, but that it would never occur to me to adopt on a perfectly serviceable bench.

126

Her bad news – and it is bad news – is that her financial situation has deteriorated. Although she still goes to sleep at her sister-in-law's, her catering duties have been taken over by students who are renting rooms in the house. Since she is no longer responsible for cooking for her sister-in-law, her monthly wages have been reduced from $20 to $10. In addition, the money from her recycling activities has gone down. Cans bring in 3500 riels per kilo instead of 4500, and there has been an even more dramatic drop in what she gets for plastic bottles and cardboard: from 1500 riels per kilo down to 400, and 1300 to 250. In each case, it takes about a week to fill one big sack, which means that what she collects over a couple of weeks is worth 6000 to 7000 riels. Less than two dollars. The only good thing – as far as I can see – is that the recycling is a sideline, a by-product of her sweeping job in the church compound. It is not her main source of income and does not require a lot of extra time.

As for the little girl who was accompanying her, she is not a granddaughter, as I had surmised. She is the daughter of one of her neighbours and is happy to come along. Her own grandchildren are with their parents in another part of the country. She has not seen them for five years.

MING LIN

At Ming Lin's suggestion, we are not meeting in the presbytery like last year, but at her house. I have been to Ming Lin's home before, a great favour I am told. She invited me to visit when her husband was still alive, probably around a year before his death, by which time his behaviour towards her had improved. What I remember most vividly from this first visit is Ming Lin telling me that they did not sleep in the main bedroom – that was their son and daughter-in-law's room – but on the floor of the landing, on a mat that was rolled away during the day. Besides being rather narrow for two people, the landing was next to a flight of stairs opening onto a void, with no handrail or any kind of balustrade in-between, and I had asked if she wasn't afraid of falling over the edge. She wasn't, and seemed quite content with the arrangements.

Major improvements have been made to the building since that time. There is a new roof and the ground floor has been concreted. Ming Lin tells us how, before this was done, the floor would flood during the rainy season and get very muddy. To make these improvements she asked the Church for a loan, which she is paying back in instalments. She tells us that she wants to work another two years to clear the debt and then retire and relax. Whether she will be able to do so is far from certain for, as she readily admits, in the absence of state pension provision, she has no idea what she would live on. Hers is a common predicament among older Cambodians and many people do their utmost to work for as long as they are physically capable in order to avoid becoming a burden on their families.

Ming Lin currently shares her house with seven family members: five adults and two children. Most of them are around when we arrive and there is a flurry of activity to locate some plastic chairs for us to sit on. I am facing the kitchen area, which bears a strong resemblance to the kind of set up we used to have when we took the family camping on holiday, with most items on show rather than hidden away in cupboards. On my right is a large bed with a television perched at the end which one of the children will remain glued to the whole time we are there. Thoughts of how nice it would be if it was switched off keep floating through my mind.

We talk about the other adults living in the house: three sons, the wife of one of the sons, and a daughter. The first son works in a crocodile farm. There are around a thousand crocodile farms in Cambodia, most of them breeding farms that export baby crocodiles for a marginal profit to neighbouring countries, typically Thailand and Vietnam. Raising crocodiles to maturity is a lucrative business. The animals will end up as luxury designer handbags that sell for thousands of pounds, but Cambodian crocodile farms generally lack the capital and technical expertise to raise the reptiles to the point, around three years of age, when their skin can be sold for a high price. Here, as in so many other cases, Cambodia lies at the bottom of the supply chain and the big money is made elsewhere. The other sons and the daughter have less exotic jobs. One of the sons sets up solar panels, the other installs lighting in houses, and the daughter, whose school fees, we are told, the Church helped to pay for, is a hairdresser/cosmetician. When we ask who has the better paid job, they all agree: the installer of solar panels.

We'd like to hear what working in a crocodile farm involves, but this will have to wait for another occasion.

CHANGES AND DEVELOPMENTS
IN 2015: CHOMNAOM

———

Chomnaom, 2016

OM RIM & TA JOK

As in Battambang, we also discuss recent developments. In the case of Om Rim and Ta Jok, recent history actually takes pride of place as, upon our arrival, Om Rim, who was expecting our visit, launches straightaway into a description of her activities over the past few weeks. She informs us that she is currently busy collecting snails in a rice field. We have tried a range of Cambodian delicacies over the years, but have never sampled the kind of large snails Om Rim is talking about. Not because we have avoided them. We simply haven't been offered any, though I must admit that I am not sure what our reaction would be if we were ever invited to taste them. I gather from a friend, who had some during a recent visit to Chomnaom, that becoming temporarily vegetarian when offered local snails may not be such a bad idea. They are not, it would appear, an unmissable culinary experience.

Before turning to gathering snails, Om Rim spent two months gleaning rice, filling a total of 12 sacks weighing 90 to 95 kilos each. Every day, she rode out in the morning to a field located 3 to 5 kilometres away and spent the whole day gleaning. This, together with the 60 sacks of rice that their own field produced, has enabled the couple to buy some extra soil in order to raise the ground level of the property. They hope this will stop their house from being flooded like the previous one was. "I work hard for my family", she says with pride.

When we came to Chomnaom last year, Om Rim and Ta Jok had just moved into their new house. A year on, I wonder how they are finding the new accommodation. They do not appear quite as enthusiastic as they were. They have partitioned off part of the first floor, which at the time of the blessing ceremony was still undivided, in order to create a bedroom. However, this is not where they sleep. After years of sleeping in an open, well-ventilated area, they find an enclosed space too dark and lacking in fresh air, a bit claustrophobic, I guess. So the bedroom is for the grandchildren.

I am reminded of a visit we paid some years ago to a girls' school run by the Salesian Sisters in Battambang. To our surprise the pupils all slept together on the top floor in an enormous dormitory. Apparently they preferred it that way. They were used to sharing a room with several other people and would have felt lonely and uncomfortable if they had their own room.

Before we leave, I ask Om Rim and Ta Jok to talk us through the pictures on the walls, and then we reciprocate by showing them photos of our family.

YIEY KOUM

Our next interview, with Yiey Koum, who has been sitting on a bench waiting for us, does not start too auspiciously. As we approach, she stands up to greet us, stumbles and nearly falls. Complaining of feeling cold, she goes round the back to fetch a shirt before lying down on the bench, reiterating that she does not feel well. Her daughter has come over to join us and we offer to come back another day, but a few minutes later Yiey Koum sits up and, somehow or other, we get on with the interview.

In the light of her evident frailty, I ask whether her daughter cooks for her. "No", the daughter replies. She used to, but Yiey Koum now insists on cooking for herself. We are told that she now has two grandchildren living with her, instead of one: the granddaughter she already took care of last year and a slightly older grandson, who seems to be quite a handful. We see him sneaking into the area at the back with a friend of his while we are talking to his grandmother, and helping himself to some drink or food. He is told not to, but she is in no position to run after him. When he returns later on, she tries in vain to persuade him to come and say hello to us. She apologises, saying that he is shy, and then adds that he is afraid of what will happen when she dies. It dawns on me that all I have ever considered, up to now, is the impact that raising their grandchildren has on the caregivers, but that the children too must be concerned about the precarious nature of the arrangements. Whether or not he is shy, Yiey Koum's grandson certainly has grounds for feeling insecure, and it would not be surprising if this contributes to his unruliness.

The most remarkable aspect of our visit is the transformation that takes place in Yiey Koum's demeanour over the course of the interview. The beginning is very much the daughter's show. Whether as a consequence of her near fall, or because this is her normal state, Yiey Koum appears lethargic, uninterested, and the daughter has to supply most of the answers. But her mother is listening and intervenes from time to time to corroborate what has been said, or, on the contrary, to make corrections. As the conversation progresses, she seems to recover some energy and becomes more animated, bending forward, for example, to illustrate being shot from behind by the Khmer Rouge. She grows more vehement in her disagreements, refusing to let her daughter have the last word. This leaves me speculating whether she is finding life dull and monotonous, whether perhaps her desire to do her own cooking is an attempt to regain and retain a degree of independence. We say good bye, pleased with the improvement in her mood, though aware it is unlikely to last long.

OM NY

Our other two interviews do not take place until a week later. We begin with Om Ny, who seems happier overall with her new house than Om Rim and Ta Jok. Yes, the upstairs can get hot during the day, but it is OK at night. Furthermore, the new building is more spacious than the old one and, importantly, offers protection against floods. Floods are rare, but are a serious problem, as the water can be as much as a foot deep.

Om Ny's family is doing well. Kimlon has been taken on by a bank not too far away and comes to visit most weekends, while the youngest daughter, whose prospects Om Ny was concerned about, has found a job in a hotel in Sihanoukville. The oldest daughter is still next door, the three sons continue to work in Thailand. They all have passports that enable them to cross the border, and they all work in the same factory, a large plant that employs Burmese and Thais as well as Cambodians. It takes some time to establish anything beyond the fact that the goods manufactured by the factory are exported to China, but eventually we come to the conclusion that what it makes has to do with car components.

We take some more pictures of the accommodation and the beautifully tended garden. With chickens wandering about and

133

plants ranging from sugar cane to bananas, oranges, papayas and mangoes, which they eat or sell, the place looks deceptively idyllic.

KROO YAT

It is then Kroo Yat's turn. Now if you had asked me last year for an example of someone making the best of not very good circumstances, the chances are that I would have said Kroo Yat. And so it comes as a shock to hear, while we are still in Battambang, that Kroo Yat has suffered a major setback. He himself makes a passing reference to what has happened, when he comes to greet us on our arrival in Chomnaom and we ask him how he is. His health is fine, he replies, but almost all his pigs have died. To supplement the income from his rice field, Kroo Yat has been raising pigs. We are not talking here of raising (and losing) the odd pig or two. We are talking of a sizeable sideline, over 30 pigs in fact, of which all bar three have died. And it all happened within the space of one week.

I lie in bed that night overcome by self-doubt and a sense of utter powerlessness at this distressing news. What's the point of coming here when things like this happen? What utopian cloud-cuckoo-land do we live in? How can we think our visits can possibly make any difference? I have an almost unbearable desire to run away. Not a reaction I often have. You have to become immune to people's troubles here and I have learnt to do that. I know that if you allow the hand-to-mouth existence, the problems of those you meet, to get to you, you will soon pack your bags and go home. But, sometimes, something still gets through your defences.

Needless to say I resist the urge to run away. I wait for morning to come, hoping, knowing, that my mood will lift when I have breakfast with the others: the students who have come to Chomnaom with us, all the people who are here to help. I know that to be with them just buoys you up. And it does.

Kroo Yat tells us more in the course of the interview: he has lost 18 small pigs weighing 20 kg each out of the 20 he had originally, all 12 of the pigs weighing 70 kg, three out of the four weighing 200kg, and a sow. These amount to a devastating blow when you consider the potential income the animals would have provided and the money he had invested in them.

They succumbed, he says, to blue ear pig disease, so called because the ears of affected pigs turn blue, with only three days separating the appearance of the first symptom and the pig's death. And it spread through the herd like lightning. He is well informed, surprisingly so given the small number of information sources at his disposal. He tells us that a number of pigs had been vaccinated but it did not seem to have made any difference. He adds that he had never encountered the disease before. He thinks it was brought by a pig farmer from the other side of the river with sick pigs, who came to find out whether Kroo Yat's pigs were OK. They seemed to be, but two days later it was a different story.

Back home I look up blue ear disease on the Internet. It turns out to be a well known, highly infectious condition, called porcine reproductive and respiratory syndrome (PRRS) that, as the name indicates, leads to reproductive failure and respiratory illness. The clinical sign of blue ears only seems to appear in a small percentage of pigs and is said to be due to the pig's body redirecting blood flow to vital organs. Blue ear pig disease was first reported in the 1980's in North America and Europe but has since crossed to China and the rest of East Asia. It is caused by a virus with a high mutation rate. I discover various descriptions of how the virus is transmitted. They list, inter alia, the movement of carrier pigs, airborne transmission up to three kilometres, and a cause of spread that particularly draws my attention, because it suggests that Kroo Yat may be right to suspect his pigs' fate to have been sealed by the farmer's visit: contaminated boots and clothing.

We see the three surviving pigs in their pens when we go to Kroo Yat's house. They are not free range in the common acceptation of the term, but they are kept protected from the sun and currently have plenty of room, although space must have been limited when there were more of them. They look healthy for now, but how will Kroo Yat recover from a loss of that magnitude?

VIP TREATMENT

Chomnaom, 2016

In between the interviews, we visit other parishioners, are shown ongoing as well as new projects, take part in religious services, go round kindergartens and schools, observe classes, do our "*Head, shoulders, knees and toes*" routine, teach in the Tep Im Centre, watch displays and shows. Our programme varies from day to day and year to year. Sometimes we follow the priests around, sometimes we strike out on our own. Everywhere we always receive a great welcome and are treated as special guests.

I am not averse to being made a fuss of. From time to time. On my birthday, for instance. However, going around like a minor royal is rather different. It is something which it has taken me a long time to come to terms with, although I am more comfortable with it nowadays than I used to be. In part, because I know the special treatment that we receive, the merrymaking that surrounds our visits, to be manifestations of Eastern hospitality. Our hosts want to show us the best there is to see so that we feel valued and appreciated. But also because it has occurred to me that there is another side, that we give as well as receive.

Those of our grandchildren who have reached the dizzy heights of primary school love it when we go and see them perform – more often than not as a shepherd in a Christmas play with their two and a half words to say. The youngsters who appear in the shows and performances we attend in Cambodia are the same – give or take two and a half words. They too get a boost from the opportunity to display their talents, to demonstrate what they are capable of.

The ability to move as gracefully as the dancers we watch – to take one example – to hold difficult poses, to work in perfect synchronisation with others, is not something acquired overnight. Behind their high standards lie long hours of practice, which, since participation is voluntary and there is no shortage of takers, one can only assume to be enjoyable and fulfilling. All  the same, to be truly meaningful and worthwhile, practice must lead to something. It needs to progress to rehearsal and then to public performance. But for this to happen, you need to have an audience. You need spectators.

That's what we are, an audience, or part of one, contributing to the event by helping meet this core requirement, this *sine qua non*, our presence – ultimately contingent as it is on all the time and effort those in front of us have put into reaching this point – both a tribute to, and a reward for, what they have achieved. One can only hope that the implicit external validation an audience provides – especially one that includes people who have come from afar – will combine with our smiles, with our clapping, and with our congratulatory remarks at the end, when the performers come and mingle, to increase their self-confidence and spur them on.

The same applies, with minor variations, to many of our activities in Cambodia. Add to this that the status of VIP is not something that you can shed. It is not a peerage. It is not a title, a position you can renounce, an honour you can refuse. It comes with the territory. You can be as reluctant a VIP as you like, you won't stop VIPness being bestowed on you, and it will stick to you like glue, the permanent kind of superglue that can't be removed. Let me illustrate with an incident we are unlikely to forget.

To be unable to join in the responses or the singing when you attend Mass in a foreign language can be frustrating. With yearly visits and a bit of effort, you may gradually learn the more common responses, which, because of their frequency and standardised nature, are relatively easy to pick up. Hymns, however, are a different matter. The tunes are not necessarily hard to learn, but the repertoire tends to be too vast to memorize the words, and you have to be a fluent reader to sing from a text you have not seen before. Michael and I don't read Khmer well enough to do that, although he is better at it than me. So we have to confine ourselves to following what people are singing in our hymn books, joining in here and there as best we can. It works fairly well, provided we can turn to the right page.

Unfortunately, because the page and number of a hymn in Chomnaom are only announced when it is about to be sung, to get to the right page before the start, you must be able to recognize numbers spoken at normal speed and know their written forms. Quite a tall order, as anyone who has learnt a foreign language will tell you, especially when the numbers are in Khmer script, not Arabic or Roman numerals. So we need help.

Here I must backtrack a little and tell you that when we first went to Chomnaom, I was both very surprised to discover that parishioners tended to spurn hymn books and very impressed by their ability to sing from memory. It was years before I found out that most parishioners were illiterate and realized that they did not have a choice. Clearly, someone who cannot read won't be able to point us to the right page, so we try to sit next to someone who can, which, in practice, means someone with a book. It is not fool proof but it works.

On the particular day I have in mind, there is hardly anybody around when we arrive for Sunday Mass. It is still quite early, and the only people in the church are two or three rows of children at the very front, some students helping with the liturgy near the altar, and a few adults at the back, including a lady with a book. We go and sit next to her and wait. A few people trickle in. Followed by a few more, most of whom go and sit down on the opposite side from us. The church looks strangely empty, with a big gap in the middle between the children and the adults. Fr Pedro, who has gone to the front, turns round and motions to those at the back to close the gap. No one moves, so we stay put. One of the students comes over and invites us to move forward. There is still no one with a book in front of us, so I assure him that we are perfectly fine where we are. He goes away. He is back a minute later: "Fr Pedro says you must move forward. There is a whole crowd of people outside behind you, but they don't want to come in and sit in front of you." Remember the parable of the guests in which Jesus advises his listeners to go and sit in the lowest seat? Well the parishioners have clearly heard it too. We strike a deal with the go-between: we will move forward, but he must come and sit next to us.

It should be stressed that you do not have to be a foreign visitor to be treated like a VIP. Anyone in the prefecture, whatever their age, gender, occupation, nationality, or religion, can find himself, or herself, promoted to "Very Important Person" in the twinkle of an eye.

It is 10 February 2015, the date of the official opening of "The Friendship Bridge". The Friendship Bridge is a narrow structure spanning the river directly in front of Chomnaom church that allows pedestrians, cyclists and motorcyclists – but not cars – to cross between the two banks without having to go further along the river to the main bridge. Made of concrete, the Friendship Bridge was funded by foreign donations – hence its name – and replaces an old wooden rickety affair that was tumbling down. It was designed by Fr Pedro, with a lane for those on two wheels and a higher lane, for safety, for those on foot. (If you have ever been on a single-lane shared-use bridge, you will know that pedestrians don't stand a chance against two-wheelers, especially motorised ones.) It was finished a while ago and has been in use for some time, but it deserves a proper opening ceremony and today is the day.

Since early morning, Kroo Yat has been playing with the public address system to ensure that its lungs are in good health. Judging by the amount of amplification they produce, they are in fine fettle. Even dangerously so, if you ask me, at least when you are having breakfast 25 metres away. "It's rather loud, I remark to Fr Pedro, isn't it?" He does not take the hint, just smiles, shrugs, and replies: "Yes, they like loud music."

The official opening is an important community event which is to be attended not only by Bishop Kike, but by an assortment of local functionaries and a group of monks from a nearby pagoda. The ceremony will not take place in the church compound, but on the opposite bank, where a marquee occupying the whole width of the lane has been erected. Red and white bunting has been hung across the compound and over the sides of the bridge, which is being swept and washed and has been decorated with pretty flower arrangements. Two wooden statues, one of the Virgin Mary, the other of St Thérèse of Lisieux, the parish's patron saint, have been brought over. They stand next to two benches, with flowers in front of them, just outside the marquee.

We stroll over as the final preparations are being made. Half of the marquee is already filled with plastic chairs, including some small seats for the kindergarten children. More plastic chairs are being brought in, before the look of the first few rows goes up a notch, thanks to the magical transformative effect of draping them with the kind of covers with ties and bows used at wedding receptions. These chairs are where ordinary VIPs will sit. The real dignitaries will be given cane seats, not plastic ones, although this does not look much of a step-up comfortwise. Bishop Kike will sit at the front, next to an official whose title I do not catch, and will be facing the people, with a small table in front of him. There is a bench on the right for the Buddhist monks. The other officials will sit on the left. A space has been left vacant for a brief display of traditional ballet by the prefecture's dance troupe. The areas where people will walk are being covered with a range of multi-coloured rugs and carpets. It all looks splendid.

People have started to arrive and we loiter at the back to greet those we know. At least that's our excuse. Fr Pedro, who is master of ceremony and has a lot resting on his shoulders, is rushing around, uncharacteristically flustered. He comes to fetch us: "Come with me and do what I say." Oops! I feel like a naughty child chastised for misbehaving. We follow him, sneaking into the second row, hoping this will do. Whether it escapes his notice or whether he is satisfied, I do not know, but he does not object.

Our choice will turn out to have been judicious, as the first row is eventually occupied by some of the lesser officials, which mercifully spares us a rerun of the "could you please move" scenario evoked above. However, you may well take a different view, and point out that, in opting to sit in the second row rather than at the very front, we unwittingly deprived ourselves of the opportunity to assess how much more embarrassing it is to be asked to move to a lower place, than to be directed to a higher one.

The ceremony is under way. There is music, as well as dancing, and a lot of long speeches. Made longer by the Cambodian custom of beginning a formal speech with individual salutations to all the truly important people present. Obviously, you have to leave yourself out, but it is no great hardship, as you can rest assured of being personally mentioned every time someone else takes the floor. It makes one hanker after "Ladies and Gentlemen".

Chanthorn and Kounny (our other interpreter) are sitting on either side of us, tasked with explaining who the speakers are and with conveying the gist of what is being said. They do their best but they have problems keeping up. Try as I may, my attention and my eyes wander. But what is this? A figure in black has appeared at the other end of the bridge, an old man with a stick, who seems to be coming in our direction. Probably someone who has come out for a little walk, to check on the water level perhaps, or maybe just to cross over. Surely, when he gets to the middle of the bridge, he will see that he can't get through and turn around. But, no, he is going on! Maybe he hasn't seen that the way is blocked. This is a shame, because he is clearly not very mobile and may have trouble getting to the place he wants to reach. I needn't worry. He does not want to get anywhere in particular. He has just heard some noise and has come out to investigate what the commotion is about. And he is clearly not going to be put off by the sight of a marquee, even one barring the way.

He is coming closer, and closer. He will soon be standing behind Bishop Kike, who remains blissfully unaware of any possible disruption to the ceremony. I am on tenterhooks.

The old man is not turned away, as he might well be somewhere else. Instead, someone stands up and goes to him. A chair is found and added to the first row, just in front of Michael, as it happens. Stealing the show, the old man is gently escorted to his seat and sits down. People pat his shoulder. The official next to him leans over, enquiring whether he is all right, or maybe explaining what is going on.

The extra guest turns out to be the oldest man in the village and, as such, entitled to some respect. In an admirable illustration of "*The last shall be first*", he is catapulted to the top of the pecking order at the end of the ceremony, and invited to begin the cutting of the red ribbon, which, in time-honoured fashion, has been strung across the bridge. An array of cameras and mobile phones, assembled to record the occasion, capture him for posterity in his moment of glory. "Click, click". "*Muy tiet, muy tiet*" (one more, one more). Compliant, if a little bemused, the gatecrasher is immortalised with his newly conferred VIP status.

TIME TO MOVE ON

———

England, 2016-2017

By the time I put the 2016 interviews into some kind of shape, most of the problems that I spotted last year have been ironed out, leaving only one or two issues in need of clarification. There is, I am sure, much more to be said about the Khmer Rouge era, but unless the topic crops up naturally, I do not intend to bring it up again. I am aware that to retrieve enough details and incidents to build a comprehensive picture of what life was like under the Khmer Rouge would require a much longer time scale than the one at our disposal, and that the iterative process involved in bringing to the surface recollections that may have laid hidden for many years has the power to cause significant emotional pain.

To go beyond what the participants have shared with us and the fleeting emotions that passed over their faces, one needs to turn to the more extensive treatment found in books written by survivors. Like all memoirs, survivors' accounts are prone to inaccuracies, distortions and exaggerations, but they still offer one of the best windows into the past available to us. They have the merit of giving us an insider's view, showing scenes and aspects of life that illustrate the unimaginable brutality of the regime and its impact on mental health and emotional well being.

One of the most informative narratives I have read is Loung Ung's autobiography *"First They Killed My Father"*, recently adapted for the screen by Angelina Jolie. Following the fate of an upper middle class family forced out of Phnom Penh by the Khmer Rouge, the book lays out the chain of events that took the author from a happy childhood in a well off family through a succession of horrifying experiences at the hands of the Khmer Rouge, to a spell in a Thai refugee camp, waiting with her eldest brother and his wife to depart for the US.

Treated like pawns in a vast chess game, the family were moved from one place to another without any idea of what lay in store for them. They were soon deprived of their possessions. In what I found to be a particularly moving scene, Ung recounts her distress at watching, at the age of five, her most cherished dress tossed on top of a pile of clothes and set alight. She describes the nightmarish existence of sheer helplessness forced on people at the mercy of pitiless supervisors ready to deny a parent permission to visit their dying child, and aptly conveys her father's anguish and sense of guilt at his inability to protect his children, and his mortification when forced to rely on one of his sons for supplementing the family's food rations.

She draws attention to causes of pain that are not obvious when you have been spared such horrors: how chronic undernourishment and long hours spent toiling in the sun take a heavy toll on your own and your loved ones' physical appearance, how sad you feel at this rapid aging.

Because Ung's father had supported the Lon Nol government, the family lived under the constant threat of his past being discovered. The children were therefore instructed to obey, to conform, and to avoid any reference to their life in Phnom Penh. We read that they were warned not to show their feelings and that, as time went on, the more vivacious and outgoing among the siblings became progressively less talkative. They withdrew into themselves and their faces became impassive.

Ung's depiction of daily life under the Khmer Rouge demonstrates that the tentacles of the regime extended to all areas of life. The severity of the Khmer Rouge rule is shown to have brought a host of hardships, from having to walk barefoot on rough terrain when you were used to wearing shoes, to living in a state of permanent uncertainty and anxiety. Fear of being reported and punished for some small infraction to the draconian edicts of a tyrannical regime bent on controlling body and mind drove people to distrust everyone. From time to time an individual, or even a whole family, would disappear, but, significantly, disappearances were never talked about. It would not have been safe to do so.

To support the leadership's ambition to re-educate their compatriots, you were required to attend hours of relentless indoctrination. The topics were always the same, and even the children seem not to have been fooled by reports of the government's professed love for the people, the unmatchable feats of Khmer Rouge soldiers, the remarkable achievements of the regime, or the equally unbelievable promises of a better future. How could you be taken in when your experience and the evidence around you belied such ridiculous claims? You knew only too well that you were being fed lies.

The violence of the Khmer Rouge made you want to retaliate, but your hatred had to be kept under control. Ung admits that she welcomed and nursed the rage she felt at all the harm done to her family. Hatred helped her to keep sad memories at bay, while the hope of coming back one day to make the perpetrators pay gave her a purpose for going on living.

Whereas Ung's background was the epitome of what the Khmer Rouge abhorred and wanted to get rid of, our own contacts were poor and less educated and, as such, more acceptable to the leadership. They also lived in a different region, where people do not appear to have been classified into "base people", or "old people" – that is to say peasants who had lived in Khmer Rouge controlled areas before 1975 – and "new people" – city dwellers, like Ung's family, who had lived under Lon Nol and were singled out for harsher treatment. In fact, when asked, our informants said they had not heard of such a distinction, although they were aware that town dwellers, unused to physical work in the open air, found it harder to cope, and that more of them died.

One can understand how, at times such as these, religious people would cling to their faith and take refuge in prayer despite the ban on worship. Not only because of the absence of any other beacon of hope, but also as a small private act of defiance, a way of making a stand, albeit secretly, against the Khmer Rouge, of asserting yourself.

What did they say when they prayed, I wonder. They asked for help, I presume, for peace to return, for strength. Perhaps, like Om Ren, they recited the Rosary. A standard form of prayer, imbued with the familiarity of the well-known, a link with an imagined community of other Catholics, some of whom might conceivably be doing the same thing as you at that very moment.

While I intend to draw a line under the Khmer Rouge era, I would like, during our next round of interviews, to revisit some aspects of life under the Vietnamese. And, of course, find out about noteworthy recent developments. These two strands form the backbone of the next part, which also includes glimpses into the rest of our trip. We learn, when we arrive, that Om Ri has gone to live in Phnom Penh after falling out with one of the other people involved in keeping the grounds tidy. We are therefore unable to find out how she has fared over the past year, though she puts in an appearance in the section on the Vietnamese occupation, thanks to some details recorded during her 2016 interview.

PART FOUR

2017

ROUND 3

————

England, 2017

Here we are again, getting ready to travel to Cambodia. This time next week, we will be on our way to Heathrow airport to catch a flight to Siem Reap via Hong Kong. We won't stop over in Hong Kong, as we spent a few days there, back in 2010, when we visited the main tourist sights. To make the most of this rare opportunity, we had booked a double room in what the guidebook described as the best guesthouse in Hong Kong. "Very central", with a "helpful staff", a description fully borne out by the emails exchanged before our visit. The guesthouse was indeed centrally located, and the staff could not have been more obliging, sending us information on what to see, how to get there, and so on. They also turned out to be great experts in expectations management.

"The room is a little small", mentioned the receptionist checking us in. As we were fully aware of the pressure on space in Hong Kong, her remark did not strike us as particularly surprising news. We would have been much more surprised if she had told us that the room was quite spacious. "The room is a little small", she repeated on the way to our accommodation, adding "but very clean", presumably to compensate for the negative impression that her previous comment might have created. She must have thought we were hard of hearing and had not caught what she had said, for she said it again. By the time we reached the end of the corridor we did not anticipate anything but a small room, the dimensions of our accommodation having gone down in our minds with each repetition of "a little small". Even so, the room we had pictured wasn't nearly as cramped as the one she opened the door onto. If "small" was accurate, "a little" was somewhat of an understatement; "incredibly" would have been nearer the truth. In fact, the room would have been a serious contender for first prize in a "smallest double bedroom in the world" competition. If you know how to fit a normal size double bed and an en-suite in an area measuring less than 2 metres by 2.3, which is what our room measured, I am sure they would like to hear from you. As Michael remarked, rather cynically I thought: "It is so clean because it is so small."

This time, we are only staying long enough in Hong Kong to switch from Cathay Pacific to Dragonair. Our travel vaccinations are up to date, we have bought our malaria tablets, and we have invested in anti-mosquito products. To Deet or not to Deet? We hesitated and then decided to hedge our bets. And, mindful of how I was bitten by mosquitoes last year, not just once but two or three times, in the few minutes it took us to cross the 100 or so metres separating the airport arrivals area and the car park, I am going to smother myself with insect repellent before even setting foot outside. Astonishingly, Michael escaped unscathed from the trip across the car park. *Normally*, as our grandchildren are prone to say when we inadvertently try and stop them from doing something their parents allow – while keeping remarkably quiet about parental behavioural norms when it is the other way round and we allow something the parents don't – *normally*, mosquitoes leave me alone and shower their affection on Michael.

However, as I have discovered to my cost, Cambodian mosquitoes belong to a different breed. Instead of paying me scant attention like their European cousins, they look upon my limbs as a kind of award winning restaurant offering a rare opportunity to sample French haute cuisine. The biggest feast I have known them to have (or at least attempt to have) was when I came on my own in August 2008. It was the rainy season, the period when going out during a downpour without a raincoat will get you soaked in less than 10 paces. The time, too, when mosquitoes are at their most virulent.

Before going to Battambang, I first went South to Chumkriel school near Kampot, where I had volunteered to teach English for a few days. I foolishly believed in those days that mosquitoes can't survive the cold. It is, after all, a popular myth. My room in Kampot had A/C so I set this at 19°C and, for added protection, rigged up a way of suspending the mosquito net I had brought with me. Quite an achievement as air-conditioned rooms don't provide hooks for hanging nets, the received wisdom being that nets are unnecessary since mosquitoes, etc. But, as I soon found out, there is a cold worshipping variety of mosquitoes that are not put off by 19°C. Worse luck, my room seemed to have been chosen as the venue for their annual convention. To be fair, they were very quiet and flew noiselessly around, but try as they might to be unobtrusive, I knew they were there. Not least because of the cool air blowing on me. I would wake up frozen in the middle of the night, get out of bed – a perilous move under the circumstances – adjust the temperature, climb back in, get too warm, turn the temperature down, get too cold again, and so on. To cap it all, it occurred to me, after four days of this ineffective rigmarole, that sleeping with a mosquito net impregnated with repellent practically next to my nose – it had been the only solution – might not be the smartest idea in the world. The net was discarded. Another dangerous move, immediately seized upon for a Michelin inspection and the unmistakable conferment of a three-star rating.

Hopefully we have the mosquito problem covered. We have ordered our dollars and, with a bit of luck, will not leave half of them behind, as we did some years ago. As usual, I have arranged to go and pick up drawings by pupils of St Mary's school in Ipswich to take to Cambodia. Every year, Class Two at St Mary's draw pictures for Samaki primary school in Chomnaom, where one of the classes reciprocates and gives us pictures to take back to St Mary's. This year we are also bringing a recording.

Following a new governmental initiative, Cambodian pupils in the final years of primary school have started learning English. As they do not have audio recordings, we brought home a copy of their textbook last year, and some of St Mary's pupils have recorded a small set of extracts, which have been put on a memory stick to take with us. Our plan is to play some of the recordings from our laptops when we are there. What happens after that is unclear as the school does not currently have computers, but they will work something out. It would be better, of course, for the two schools to have an audio link, but, given the conditions in Chomnaom, such a prospect looks only marginally less remote than a delivery service using flying pigs.

We have bought a few presents and put together an assortment of photos to show or give away. I have reread what I've written for this book, identified a few gaps, a few issues to probe into, some new topics to investigate. We have not packed yet, but we have printed a list of what we will need to take with us. The usual routine.

Except that this trip is not entirely usual. For the first time ever, we won't be meeting up with Fr Pedro, who has been so supportive, so helpful these past nine years. He is off to Canada for what is likely to be a long sabbatical. We will miss him. His duties are being taken over by other priests, so we are not going into totally new and unfamiliar territory. We know the ropes, we speak a little Khmer, we will manage, but it won't be the same.

We have known since last year that Fr Pedro would not be there. And while part of me wishes that things had not changed, in recent weeks I have come to regard his absence as underscoring that the main purpose of our visits is not to renew and develop our friendship with the priests, who tend to move around, but with the communities with which St Mary's is twinned. As I was writing up the interviews, I kept wondering how people had fared since last year. Has Kroo Yat got some new pigs? Has Om Ren's grandson been accepted into the new centre for people with learning difficulties? To see our contacts again is a prospect I am genuinely looking forward to.

TRAVELLING FUN

———

February 2017

17 February 2017. We took a coach down to London earlier
today and are staying overnight in a hotel on the Bath Road
to get to Heathrow airport in good time tomorrow morning.
Which we do without encountering any problems. Everything
is fine, apart from the fact that the seats we have been allocated
are not next to each other. They are duly changed by the check-
in staff and we go through Security. The departure gate is not
yet up on the screens adorning the departure lounge, but will be
displayed around 10.30. Or so the screens confidently predict.
Until all references to the gate are abruptly replaced by "Flight
delayed until 12.00". We don't have long to change planes in
Hong Kong, but our departure has only been postponed by half
an hour. We figure that the plane should be able to make up the
time.

Embarkation takes place promptly at 12.00. By 2 pm, the
good news is that we have been served lunch. The not-so-good
news is that the plane is still on the tarmac. Apparently, we do
not have our full complement of pilots. We need three pilots

and are missing not one of them, but two, and, without these two pilots, we are not going anywhere. As can easily be checked by looking out of the window. I have heard announcements about waiting for passengers before, but waiting for pilots is a novelty. The reason for their absence has not been explained. Is it the result of an oversight, a failure to contact the right number of pilots? Perhaps the company, anxious to cut costs and having heard of driverless cars, decided that a single pilot and an autopilot system should be enough, but has since had second thoughts.

The reality is more banal. The missing pilots are stuck in traffic. One, then the other, eventually extricates himself (or herself?) from the perverse vehicles conspiring against them and we take to the air, four hours behind schedule.

By now, Michael and I have abandoned all hope of making the connecting flight to Siem Reap, but I haven't been idle. Taking advantage of our continuing presence on the ground, I have found out, with the help of my mobile phone,

- That Dragonair (which we are booked on for the second leg of the journey) only runs one direct flight from Hong Kong to Siem Reap per day.
- That tomorrow's flight is in the afternoon and arrives later than the last bus to Battambang.
- That, without exception, the few direct flights between Hong Kong and Siem Reap of other airlines will have departed by the time we get to Hong Kong.

We are not the only ones facing this kind of problem. Hong Kong airport is an international hub. Most of the passengers onboard are flying on to other destinations and, like us, the majority will miss their connection. Not a happy state of affairs, although our common misfortune creates a great spirit of camaraderie and gives us something to talk about as we queue for the toilets.

In Hong Kong we are transferred to a flight via Hanoi. By the time we eventually land in Siem Reap, the bus we were booked on is already in Battambang. On the plus side, since we had tickets to go straight to Battambang, Cathay Pacific have agreed to put us up in a hotel and buy us new bus tickets. They have even made arrangements for us to be picked up at 7 am to get to the bus station for 7.30.

We go down to the lobby the next morning well before 7 am. 7 am goes by with no pickup van in sight. 10 minutes go by. There is still no sign of our van. We have been to Cambodia before and know there is no reason to panic, but we think it prudent to go and ask the receptionist to check that our transport has indeed been dispatched. It has. When 7.15 turns into 7.20 without it materialising, I make another trip to the front desk. The receptionist is adamant that someone is definitely coming. We should just sit in the lobby and relax. I get the distinct impression that she regards us as seriously psychotic. We might well be, nevertheless we prefer to go and wait outside. It will save time if the van ever turns up. Without any warning, at 7.25, the receptionist runs out of the lobby and announces that we need to go all the way down to the road. She thinks she can see our pickup, over there, some 100 yards away on the other side of the busy dual carriageway. It is indeed our pickup, but by now it is also 7.30 and we have literally missed the bus.

There follows a discovery tour of the countryside around Siem Reap during which the van driver spends most of the time with one hand on the steering wheel and the other holding his mobile to his ear. We are sitting behind him so have a pretty good view of what he is doing, but we can only hear his side of the conversation. Naturally enough, he is speaking Khmer. We can't understand what he is saying, but we infer from titbits like "the road", "Where shall I go?", that he is asking for directions to an unknown location – unknown, it would appear, not only to us but also to him – where, presumably, we will be able to climb aboard our bus. We had steeled ourselves for travelling at full speed. To our surprise, we are crawling along, in areas we have never been to, at a pace only marginally faster than when we were stuck waiting for pilots at Heathrow. Neither of us feeling inclined to just sit back and enjoy the scenery, we discuss what is going on at some length, and come to the conclusion that the bus is actually behind us, and our slow progress is designed to let it catch up with us.

At this point the driver pulls over to make yet another phone call, during which we notice that he is no longer calling his interlocutor *Bong* (older brother), the term you use when speaking to someone a little older than you, whether a relative or not, but – don't laugh – *Poo* (uncle). This seems to us a good omen, suggesting that he is talking to someone of greater seniority, and, with a bit of luck, greater knowledge and authority.

Then everything changes. In the twinkling of an eye we have turned around and are speeding back to where we left the main road. The whole thing reminds me of the Neuro Linguistic Programming rewind technique for getting rid of phobias, which involves imagining your life rewinding swiftly to before the event that triggered the phobia. With the difference that we are moving physically rather than in our imagination, and are going forwards, not backwards. In other circumstances, we might want to compare the different perspective offered by travelling super fast in the opposite direction, how the view on the way back differs from the view on the way in, but we don't feel in the mood. We decide from our driver's haste that the bus must be ahead after all. We are right. A few minutes later, we come upon a bus waiting on the side of the road in the middle of nowhere.

I am not making this up, honest, but I must admit that there are moments when even my taste for adventure does not seem quite up to the task.

LIFE AFTER THE ARRIVAL OF THE VIETNAMESE: INTERVIEWS IN BATTAMBANG AND CHOMNAOM

—

Cambodia, 2017

VISITS TO REFUGEE CAMPS

In 2015, Om Ri told us how, 18 months after returning to Battambang, she gave up her work as a seamstress and, leaving her young son behind in her sister's care, started travelling to Thailand with her mother-in-law. I was intrigued by her decision. When we met last year, I enquired what had prompted her to undertake this new venture. She replied that she wanted to earn money by buying goods to sell in refugee camps. Presumably it seemed to her to promise greater financial rewards than sewing clothes.

It was a form of trading that called for a lot of walking. First, you had to go and get suitable merchandise. Next, you had to take this to a camp. It meant sleeping on the side of the road and you ran the risk of being arrested, robbed, killed even. She gesticulated to show how there would be artillery flying around. For two women to travel by themselves seemed to me rather dangerous, so I asked whether there might not have been safety in numbers. Quite the opposite, according to her. Thai soldiers attacked groups, killed them, and then covered the bodies with branches. She never went with a group, only with her mother-in-law. I take it they deemed it easier for two women to avoid detection. However, their luck eventually ran out, when her mother-in-law was shot in the leg by Thai soldiers, who stole their goods. The injury was not fatal and Om Ri managed to get her wounded relative to Khao-I-Dang (KID), a large camp situated a few kilometres inside Thailand.

Om Ri was not the only one of our interviewees to visit refugee camps. Several of our contacts in Chomnaom reported having done this, albeit for a variety of reasons, or had family members who did. One of them is Kroo Yat who, unlike Om Ri, travelled with a group. It was a large group, he says, comprising around thirty people. They would set off at 7 am and walk until around 4 pm to get rice provided by UNICEF and bring this back to Chomnaom. He adds that they would sometimes encounter a Vietnamese road block and would have to find somewhere to sleep before carrying on.

I don't know whether Yiey Koum's husband was part of the same group, but we heard in 2015 that he, too, went to a camp to get rice in order to provide for his family, who, as we have seen, did not have anything to live on when they returned home. A brother of Kroo Yat's, who had a cart, sometimes came with him. The cart enabled them to bring back up to 300 kilos of rice. When he was on foot, Kroo Yat could only carry 15 kilos, and he would occasionally trade some of the rice he had obtained for clothes or seasoning. He says the Vietnamese soldiers in the area were not interested in the rice, but they might seize the clothes or the seasoning that people had, and any woman in the group risked being raped.

In contrast to the others, Om Ren did not just go to visit a refugee camp. She actually took the family to live in one.

Worried that the husband might be arrested by the Vietnamese if they found out that he had been a soldier in the Cambodian army, the couple decided to pack all their belongings and set out in the direction of the Thai border. There were lots of people on the move, she recounts, some just walking, some with a cow cart, and some, like her, pushing a bicycle. It reminds me of my mother's description of 'L'Exode', the period in May-June 1940 in France when millions of people fled South ahead of the advancing German army.

It took Om Ren and her husband three days to reach their destination: Site 2, the largest refugee camp on the Thai-Cambodian border. On the way, they slept under a tent on the side of the road at night, first near Sway Sisophon, and then in Nimitt, the place where Om Rim lived after moving to the North West.

The family would spend 13 years in Site 2. When I enquire why they stayed so long, she replies that Battambang was full of Vietnamese and that they were afraid to return because of her husband's past. Some people went back earlier, but they felt it would not be safe for them to go back to Battambang. And so the camp became their life, as indicated by some of the pictures displayed around the room we are currently sitting in: Om Ren's husband at a welcoming ceremony for a bishop from Rome some time around 1984-86, catechists in Site 2, another priest in Site 2 whom she calls Père Pierre.

I wonder what everyday life was like in a refugee camp. I have looked at works discussing the dubious status of the string of camps scattered along the Thai-Cambodian border. I am aware that there were military camps controlled by the Khmer Rouge as well as camps like Site 2 under the control of KPNLF, the Khmer People's National Liberation Front, which opposed the People's Republic of Kampuchea regime (PRK) installed by the Vietnamese. I have learnt that Khao-I-Dang, the camp Om

Ri took her mother-in-law to, was a holding camp for refugees who were to be resettled abroad, and was run by the UNHCR (United Nations Human Rights Council). I have read about the pressures exerted by conflicting ambitions, opposing factions and vested interests, and the difficulties encountered by aid agencies trying to channel humanitarian aid to people. What I have yet to see is detailed descriptions of the residents' lives.

Like many people, I suspect, I imagine a hand-to-mouth existence, especially at first, fraught with dangers. After all that people had lived through, to deal with the substance of ordinary life, the feeding and clothing of children, the task of bringing them up as well as possible without entirely neglecting your own needs, must have come as a relief. Still, you were not back in your own home.

I find some insights into camp life in a biography of Bishop Kike, Battambang's apostolic prefect, whom we have met many times over the last ten years. Like a child looking incredulously at old pictures of earlier versions of people she knows, I discover in *The Heart of the Lonely Tree* by Rodríguez Olaizola, a Kike before Bishop Kike, a Kike before Fr Kike even, one who has no idea as yet that his life will dance in and out of Cambodian stories before finally taking its place among them.

Kike's introduction to Cambodia, at the age of 26, could hardly have been more dramatic. Here is part of the description he gave during an interview for the weekly radio and television program *Where God Weeps* of his arrival at a Cambodian refugee camp in 1985:

- You arrived in Cambodia in 1985, when it was at war. What was your first impression?

- First fear, I was dying of fear. When I went to the refugee camps it was an odyssey. One had to pass five military controls, and every time one was passed, things became darker: military men dressed in black, not smiling, asking for one's papers in a violent way. When I arrived at the gate of the refugee camp, I shall never forget it, the level-crossing opened and we went in. Before me, all of a sudden, were the children, very badly dressed, barefoot but joyful! I recall much joy, life ... life ... life, life in plenitude although they were shut in in a refugee camp, let's say, as prisoners of war.

–   And what happened next?

–   Then I went to visit them and I was received by Jhaimet, who was like their leader. I remember very well: He was standing with his crutches, he was missing a leg, the other one was badly wounded and he was missing an eye. I did not speak Cambodian, but there was a boy who translated for me. He said: "I have heard that you have come to help us," and I, dying of fear, said, "Yes, yes." And he said: "Well don't worry, I'll tell you what we need." At that instant I felt an immense peace, so to speak, Jhaimet was the voice of God who was saying to me: "Don't worry; here we welcome you, we love you."

(Figaredo, 2012)

Everyday life, in places like Site 2, turns out to have been not so very different from life outside. As Olaizola Rodríguez points out, many of us – myself included, I admit – have a flawed understanding of what the border camps were like. We assume that the refugees lived in tents and spent their time waiting for food, but Site 2, with its population of up to 180 000 people, was like a small city. The inhabitants, mostly women and children, lived in simple cabins, which improved as time went on, and went about the normal activities of daily life. The children went to school. People bought and sold goods. There were places dispensing food and medicines, a hospital, offices, cinemas and radio stations, people riding on bikes and then motorbikes. But there was also overcrowding, dissension, alcoholism. The relative normalcy of life helps explain why Om Ren and her family chose to stay there so long. And also, maybe, why she does not feel the need to describe what life was like.

LIFE IN BATTAMBANG AND CHOMNAOM

Meanwhile, those of our contacts who stayed in Battambang or Chomnaom were beginning to rebuild their lives. Evidently, it wasn't just a question of picking up where you left off, since, as Om Pranya's story exemplifies, what awaited you on your return was not what you had left. Afraid that she might not get her house back unless she came home immediately after the defeat of the Khmer Rouge, Om Pranya returned to Battambang on 7 January 1979. Events showed her fears to be justified, as she found the house occupied by "relatives of Pol Pot soldiers". Fortunately, the strangers, the unwelcome squatters, appear to have accepted that the house truly belonged to her when she enquired what had happened to a coconut tree that they had cut down. They agreed to leave, and the family were able to move back in. But the house had been badly damaged and had to be rebuilt.

Not everyone had a house to return to or be concerned about, but to go back to the place where you had lived before made sense, especially if, like Om Borei, you had been brought up among Vietnamese sisters and could speak Vietnamese.

One major change for the few practising Catholics who came back to Battambang or Chomnaom after the overthrow of the Republic of Democratic Kampuchea was the void created by the expulsion and extermination of the clergy and the destruction of churches. Catholics were not the only religious group to be persecuted during that grim period. Buddhists suffered a similar fate. Statues of Buddha were smashed, books were burned, pagodas were destroyed or turned into warehouses or prisons. The exact death toll among Buddhist monks is unknown, but, according to a study published by the Federal Research Division of the Library of Congress, it has been estimated that as many as 50 000 monks lost their lives during the Khmer Rouge regime (Ross, 1990, p. 117). However, the regime change that took place in 1979 in the wake of the Vietnamese occupation would bring about a gradual restoration of Buddhism, whereas open practice of Christianity was to remain forbidden until 1990.

In the absence of clergy, nuns, and churches, the laity managed as best they could. Thus Om Borei tells us that she and Om Pranya got together to celebrate Christmas. One by one, in 1980 or 1981, some of the Providence sisters who had taken refuge in Vietnam started coming back. They led prayers and organised catechism classes.

It would be several years, however, before Catholics were visited by ordained priests. Such visits were rare and short. The first priest to come to Battambang seems to have been a Vietnamese priest called Fr Dao, who stayed for 2 weeks. Om Pranya dates the visit to 1989, whereas Om Borei places it in 1987-88. There were also brief visits by French missionaries, for instance Fr Emile Destombes, who had been expelled from Cambodia in 1975 and was to become Bishop of Phnom Penh. The first clerical presence to last more than a few days would not occur until 1992, when a French priest, Fr Bernard Dupraz, settled in Battambang. Fr Bernard, who stayed seven or eight years, played a seminal role in the rebuilding of the Church. He brought the Catholic community together and led it, founded a seminary, and attended to the reconstruction of Chomnaom church. Finally, after a gap of 25 years, Battambang was given a new bishop with the appointment of Bishop Kike as the successor to Mgr Tep Im.

LOOKING BACK OVER 2016:
BATTAMBANG

———

Battambang, 2017

OM PRANYA

"*Plus ça change, plus c'est la même chose*", say the French: the more things change, the more they stay the same. A fatalistic epigram about the illusory, superficial nature of change and its lack of impact on important matters. Whatever apparent progress may seem to have been made over the past few months, years, or decades, when you scratch the surface, you will find the same issues as before, the same fundamental injustices and inequalities, masked, perhaps, but there, nonetheless, when you dig a bit deeper, as history repeats itself again and again.

This is certainly my impression as we listen to our interviewees talking about the past year and their current circumstances. There have been improvements here and there, but there have also been setbacks, so that what comes over is the impression of a perpetual struggle to make ends meet.

In Om Pranya's case, there has been no improvement whatsoever. In fact, she has experienced another bereavement:

the loss of a sister, who was her only remaining sibling. "*Ma soeur est décédée, le 8 décembre 2016*", she says, as we arrive.

I have a clear recollection of being introduced to Om Pranya's sister, who, by the time we met her, had become an invalid and lived in a small house behind Om Pranya's home. We had brought some French candied fruit with us to Cambodia and had been handing them around to the people we visited. A treat, something you could not get locally, which we thought they would like. Only a handful remained when we got to Om Pranya's, and all there was left, by the time her grandchildren had helped themselves, was one single piece of candied fruit. "Let us take this to my sister", Om Pranya said, instead of picking the sweet up and putting it in her mouth. Mindful of how few good things came her sibling's way, she proceeded to lead us to a small hut at the back, where her sister was sitting on the floor, and handed her the piece of candied fruit.

Once we get going, Om Pranya is as voluble as ever. When I ask her whether or not her husband was supposed to go to Battambang airport to meet the King, she does not answer with a simple yes or no and a short explanation, but embarks on a full-blown 20 minute review of the Khmer Rouge's first few days in the city. Engrossed in her narrative, seemingly oblivious to the fact that we can't understand, she rushes on, speaking continuously for up to three minutes at a stretch. I know, I can't resist timing her covertly. Chanthorn tries vainly to stop her, looks at us, smiles and shakes his head. After a while, he has another go, and another, eventually managing to get her to pause, but no sooner has he finished clarifying and translating what she said than she is off again.

I do get my answer. No, her husband did not have to go and meet the King. That particular order related to the period between 17 and 23 April. On the other hand, he should have gone to the airport at 6 am on the 24 April, like all the other men, but he happened to be in a coffee bar when the command came. He returned home ready to obey, but suspecting that the high ranking officers summoned to meet the King had been killed, since they had not been seen again, Om Pranya persuaded him not to. The clarification over, the conversation moves on to the evacuation of Battambang, with Om Pranya mimicking soldiers shooting in the air or driving people out by pointing in one direction then another.

When we start discussing the present, she confirms that yes, there is running water in the house. I am facing in a different direction from previous years, and I can see a shower cubicle on the other side of a narrow corridor. She tells us that running water was installed some years ago with money borrowed from a micro-finance scheme, that it is metered and costs 1,500 riels per m³ (approximately 40 cents), that her water consumption hovers around 10m³ per month, and that her average bill is $5.

The house also has a WC. Not a sitting down one, but the type that the British attribute to the French (a "French toilet") and the French, who call squat toilets *des toilettes à la turque*, attribute to the Turks, who, for all I know, may well, in turn, pass the baton to someone else. Squat toilets are fine when you are young, says Om Pranya, but not when your leg muscles are getting weak, especially if, as is the case here, there is no handrail nearby to hang on to. I ask whether the toilet is connected to a sewer. It is not, but there is a septic tank under the floor, which is emptied every five years.

From the water supply we pass effortlessly to other utilities, or rather, to the one other utility that she has, namely electricity. She paid $200-300 to have electricity installed (against $325 for installing running water), it costs 780 riels per kilowatt, and her monthly bill comes to $15. As for the rubbish, it is collected by the municipality. The charge for this is $1 per month.

All these sums may seem rather small, but so is her consumption of water and electricity, and even relatively modest charges can represent a major drain when you don't have much money to live on. What method does she use to pay, I ask, not expecting, naturally, something as sophisticated as direct debit, just someone coming round to collect the money. No, no one comes round. Every month she must go and pay the bills in an office in Battambang.

OM REN

Our next appointment is with Om Ren. We know where she lives, we have been to her house before, but what we find when we get there baffles us. Surely this is the right address, but where is the house? It is there, actually, though hidden, and it has changed beyond all recognition. The familiar dwelling has gone and has been replaced by something much more grand, quite splendid indeed. "I have a new house", she proudly informs us, as if this needed pointing out, when she comes to unlock the garden gate. We are pleased for her. The previous building was certainly ripe for modernisation, as the phrase goes. However, the sharp contrast between Om Ren's new abode, which cost $28 000 to build, and its neighbours is a little worrying, and looks to us like a potential stumbling block to trouble-free relationships.

Not that this is the only new house on the block. Here and there, flimsy structures have become solid buildings nestling behind unmistakable markers of territoriality. As if growing affluence propelled people towards enclosure. As if it required the easy going, fluid limits of the past to be replaced with fences, walls, and gates proclaiming: "This is mine." It gives the neighbourhood a markedly different look and feel.

Om Ren describes how the remodelling was a family affair. The costs were borne by her Australian son-in-law, after his wife came to visit and saw the poor state of her mother's house. The new home was designed and built by one of her sons, a hotel manager who, she says, learnt the necessary skills from his own son, who is a professional engineer. A case of knowledge being passed up rather than down. Like when your eight-year-old granddaughter shows you how to use your mobile phone to take videos.

Before we have time to rejoice at Ren's good fortune, another of her sons comes in. She explains that he recently came back to live with her after getting divorced and is not coping at all well.

We continue, or would do, if Chanthorn was translating what Ren is saying. But he remains silent. I ask: "What is she saying?" "I have no idea", he replies, "she is not making any sense, she is talking of carrying a cross but there is no cross around." Chanthorn has spent several years in the Tep Im Centre, but he is not a Catholic and has not realised that Om Ren is talking metaphorically. "Oh I know what she means", I tell him, and explain. Meanwhile, Om Ren has got up and left the room. She returns holding a large poster given to her by Fr Pedro before he went away, with a large cross and a Biblical quote in Spanish that says:

"*El que quiera seguirme*
Tome su cruz y sigue"
(Whoever wishes to follow me
Let them take up their cross and follow).

Then it is back once more to the vexed question of our interviewee's age. I did some more maths when writing up the latest batch of conversations and noticed a problem. In 2015, Om Ren told us that she was born in 1947 and got married at the age of 23. However, her 2016 interview placed her wedding in or around 1963, when people born in 1947 were 16. This is most odd, especially coming from someone who can read and write and has been teaching herself English. I ask again when she was born. She now says 1945, which admittedly is a step in the right direction, but, as I point out, people born in 1945 were 18 in 1963, not 23. She considers the discrepancy. Well, she is a bit hazy about the date of her wedding, but, on the other hand, she is absolutely sure of being 75. Admittedly, her identity card gives her date of birth as 1945, but then it also shows her as having been born on 4 August, when in fact she was born in March. That seems rather a lot of errors for one identity card, but she is certain that both the year and the month on the card are wrong.

The mistake on the year looks like a simple clerical error. The substitution of August for March is more puzzling, but she thinks she knows what happened. It is common practice in colloquial Khmer to refer to months by their number in the year rather than by their official name. In other words, instead of saying "I was born in March", you say "I was born in month 3". In the same way, you say "in month 8" rather than "in August". Now, while *three* and *eight* sound very different in English, there is enough similarity in Khmer between these two numbers for one to be mistaken for the other. Khmer uses a bi-quinary counting system, a system in which only the numbers 1 to 5 have their own names, the numbers 6 to 9 being made up of 5 followed respectively by 1, 2, 3 or 4. 5 in Khmer is *pram*, 3 is *bei*, so 8 is *pram bei*. Om Ren believes that the rogue *pram* was introduced by a clerk who misheard what she was saying and wrote down *pram bei*, when what she had said was *bei*. A plausible explanation, that implies that the information entered on her identity card came from her.

If relying on private citizens to tell you what to record on official documents strikes you as rather unorthodox, bear in mind that Cambodia's civil registration records – which, in any case, are unlikely to have covered the whole population – were destroyed under the Khmer Rouge. People, in the 21st century, need a means of proving their identity, so Cambodia has had to develop a brand new set of identity papers from scratch. What is your best source of information in the absence of register evidence if not the individuals concerned? What they know may well be patchy and not entirely reliable, but what better alternative do you have? Factor in hard pressed clerks faced with processing thousands of people, and a population more used to the Khmer calendar than to the Gregorian calendar, and the occurrence of errors and inconsistencies appears a great deal less extraordinary than it does at first sight.

So which year was Om Ren actually born in? The most likely candidate seems to be 1941, which fits in with her being 75 in February 2017 and with her wedding having taken place around 1963. However, it is only a best guesstimate.

Om Ren has some more good news: the mother of the two granddaughters who were staying with her has got married to her German fiancé. She has taken back her daughters, who are learning German prior to the whole family moving to Germany. On the other hand, although her grandson was accepted by the newly opened centre for mentally disabled children, he did not settle. He can't stay still and is once more in her care virtually 24/7. *"Plus ça change ..."*

Out of the blue, as we are leaving, Om Ren mentions how much she appreciates our taking notes. We are not her only visitors, but we are the only ones to write things down. I suppose she sees this as indicating that we are genuinely interested in what she has to tell. We are, but given my earlier qualms, I find it reassuring to hear that she values the interviews.

OM BOREI

More changes are waiting for us the next day at Om Borei's house. We take our places in the garden at the front of the house. Om Borei and Michael are sharing a garden swing seat. Chanthorn and I have been given moulded plastic chairs intended for children. It is a bit of a tight squeeze, but the chairs are sturdy and do not collapse under us as I feared they might. The computers that used to be set under the porch are nowhere to be seen. Om Borei explains that her daughter and son-in-law were only *running* the Internet café that we saw. The computers weren't theirs. They belonged to a friend, who has since transferred them to another location.

Apart from that, Magkara is still working as a nurse for an NGO (Non Governmental Organisation), but her husband is currently unemployed after stopping work to take care of his dying father. Om Borei's own life is much the same as before. She still visits hospital patients, going there by motodop, which involves riding pillion on a motorbike, and continues to give alms to the poorest. Acts of charity that make you think of the well-known lines attributed to St Teresa of Avila:

Christ has no body now but yours,
No hands, no feet on earth but yours, [...]
Yours are the feet with which Christ walks to do good.

MING LIN

Due to some misunderstanding, Ming Lin is not at home when we get to her house, but she arrives a few minutes later. The temperature is 32°C and everyone's face is covered in sweat. All around us are visible signs of change, definite improvements to the living conditions. There is running water from the mains, a shower, as yet without a roof, and a toilet. There are also no less than three septic tanks, two in the yard at the front and the other under the toilet. Here too the money has come from Australia, albeit from a benefactor rather than a relative. A connection fee of $350 was paid to the local authorities, the materials cost $150, and everything was installed by one of Ming Lin's sons. The water is not drinkable, but its ready availability makes life a good deal easier. "How many people now have running water around here?" we enquire. They think about 95%, much more than before.

I have found it very puzzling that the people we interview claim to know how old they are, and yet are often unable to say which year they were born in. My own memory may not be as good as it was, but my date of birth is not something I have ever forgotten. On the other hand, I find it hard to keep track of my age, let alone everyone else's. I am about to find out how Cambodians do it.

Producing her new identity card, Ming Lin volunteers the information that it does not tally with the one she used to have. According to the old card she was born in 1950, whereas the new card shows her year of birth as 1956. She finds this a great source of merriment – well, at our kind of age, who would not be pleased to have six years taken away like this? – and mimes her surprise when she discovered the discrepancy. What I want to know, though, is how she knows her age. It is quite simple really: she knows that she was born in the year of the snake.

Ah Ah! So this is how they do it! Like the Chinese, the Khmer use a calendar based on a cycle of 12 lunar years, each associated with a particular animal. You were born in the year of the rat, or the ox, tiger, rabbit, dragon, snake, horse, goat, monkey, rooster, dog or pig. This means that all you need to know to calculate your age is: your animal year, the current animal year (the rooster in 2017), how many cycles you have lived through, and the order in which the animals appear. As Michael says: "It is like pounds, shillings and pence; as long as you can live with 12s, you're fine." The last year of the snake was 2013, which makes Ming Lin 64 (or going on to 64, depending on the month she was born in).

You may feel like objecting that [...]. I know. Take away 64 from 2017 and you get 1953, which is neither 1950, nor 1956. On the other hand, 1953 does have the merit of lying in-between 1950 and 1956. On the exact mid point, actually, like some of the compromises settling territorial disputes.

The fact is that to convert dates from the Chinese or Khmer calendar to the Gregorian calendar, and vice versa, has much to offer to nerds in search of a new hobby. Consider the following:

- The Chinese New Year moves around from year to year: the year of the snake, for instance, began on 14 February 1953, but ended on 2 February 1954.
- The Cambodian New Year, however, follows the pattern found in many other Southeast Asian cultures and falls on 13 or 14 April.
- Cambodian people do not celebrate birthdays (or at least did not use to).
- Whatever your date of birth, tradition views you as being one year old from the moment you emerge from the womb, until you become two along with the rest of your cohort when everyone's age is incremented by one in April.

No wonder people get muddled. Indeed, readers endowed with an exceptional memory will recall that back in 2015, i.e. two years ago, Ming Lin, who now claims to be 64 (or going on to 64), gave her age as 63. Let us not be pedantic about a year or two: 63/64 is in the right ball park.

Leaving the intricacies of calendars behind, we seize the opportunity to explore the weird and wonderful world of crocodiles. There are, as it turns out, two experts on hand. The son who works at the crocodile farm, and another son, equally knowledgeable, who is employed seasonally and will take over our initiation when his brother leaves, disgusted, perhaps, at our ignorance, or, more likely, called away by some mundane occupation such as going to work.

Before handing over to her sons, Ming Lin explains that the crocodile farm is situated 10 minutes or so away by motorbike and that the main job of expert number one is to collect crocodile eggs using a wood clamp to ensure the crocodiles' mouths remain shut. "How big are the crocodiles?" Ming Lin puts her hands about 60cm apart. "Oh not that big!", I say. Wrong. What

she is showing us is the width of a female crocodile head, not the animal's overall length.

The first son then provides technical details, such as what crocodiles eat: mostly fish heads (imported from Thailand), but also rats from the rice fields and snakes from the Tonle Sap, some dead, some alive. He explains that crocodiles hatch between February and June, that female crocodiles produce between 20 and 50 eggs each, and that a clutch takes an hour to collect. Beforehand, however, the pregnant females must be transferred to special cells and he has to go into the pool enclosure to help move them. This does not seem to worry him in the least: they know him and won't attack him – a sort of "they won't bite the hand that feeds them", maybe? I would not be quite so sure personally.

It is then the turn of expert number two, who does admit to having been bitten, though not seriously. He elaborates on what his brother said, explaining that there is not enough space in the farm to let the crocodiles lay eggs and hatch naturally, and that the eggs remain 40 days in the ground before hatching.

Would we like to visit? You bet! We jump at the chance.

CROCODILE FARM

Battambang, February 2017

Early the next day we find ourselves riding in a tuk-tuk, on our way to the crocodile farm where Ming Lin's sons work. Chanthorn, who is a reserved kind of person not prone to confidences, shares that he has never been to a crocodile farm and is quite looking forward to the visit. He does not say anything about it making a pleasant change from our ordinary interviews, but I guess that may well be another reason for his unusually expansive mood. Not wanting to be left out of the fun, the tuk-tuk driver, who has never visited a crocodile farm either, decides he might as well tag along rather than wait for us outside. The crocodile farm is in a quiet suburb, his tuk-tuk will be quite safe.

We park opposite a small nondescript metal backdoor set in the perimeter wall of the crocodile farm. Soon the door is unlocked and Ming Lin's son steps out, as arranged, to lead our little band of crocophiles into the promised land. We all troop in eagerly behind him as he winds his way between a motley collection of old buildings that seem to be used to store miscellaneous items of machinery. It is all very low key and unexciting until we reach a short flight of steps at the top of which our first view of the crocodile pens awaits. Not directly ahead, at our level, but some 2 metres below.

It is a striking scene, vaguely reminiscent of looking from a first or second floor balcony at holiday makers relaxing around a popular hotel pool. Minus sun loungers and parasols. Like their human counterparts, some creatures are just enjoying the sun, while others have taken refuge in the shade, in small groups or on their own, depending on how sociable they feel. From time to time a particular specimen decides to go and take a dip to cool off, scrambles over the others, and comes back suitably refreshed. Some of these more active individuals slide in the water silently, but others make a splash that you would have to be very deaf not to hear. Male crocs do this to impress the females, our guide tells us. You know, cross species characteristics never cease to amaze me.

The sky is blue, the temperature not too hot yet, everything is fine, until, suddenly, Ming Lin's son feels the urge to tell us that crocodiles living in the wild can reach up as high as where we are standing. Information we could have done without. At this piece of news, the distance between the crocodiles and us, which, in our naivety, we had looked upon as a guarantee of total safety, shrinks at a dizzying speed. Our leader is quick to reassure us: these are not wild crocodiles, they are tame crocodiles, they are well fed, why should they reach up? Why indeed? What could possibly go wrong? Undaunted, we carry on.

Pointing at a particular individual, he informs us that this is a female. "How do you tell a female crocodile from a male?" I enquire. Well, the main sign is size: according to him, the females are smaller, though I must say that this particular specimen looks pretty big to me. And the skin is not quite the same. There must be other differences, but he wisely chooses to sidestep them. He has told us enough anyway to be getting along with, and we spend part of the rest of the visit identifying which of the crocodiles are male and which are female, while he nods approvingly, pleased with our keenness to apply our newly acquired knowledge.

Learning does not come much more enjoyable than this. Not only are we picking up interesting information about crocodiles, but the learning environment is perfect: small group teaching, in situ, approachable teacher, not to mention the added thrill of lurking danger. I know the crocodiles are tame and well fed, but I would not want to trip over and see – or possibly not – what happens when you fall down among them. Even if they resist taking a bite, you can't be sure you won't be in the way if they happen to swish their tail. Which, according to our tutor, produces a force of a ton and, as we get the opportunity to observe in the course of our tour, makes quite a racket.

We go round a series of pools including a pool for baby crocodiles, fascinated by what we learn. That the skins are exported to China, Thailand and Vietnam. That crocodiles don't like vegetables. That their eggs are the size of duck eggs. That there are teeth on the ground because their teeth break off when they attack each other. That, if one of them gets accidentally killed, it gets sold for its meat. Crocodile meat would seem to be a highly prized delicacy in Cambodia. There is no shortage of eager customers, we are told, from restaurants in Siem Reap or Phnom Penh to the people in neighbouring houses. A kilo of boneless crocodile will set you back by a handsome $10, but, if you can't afford this and want a cheaper deal, then go for crocodile with the bones in at $5 a kilo. In fact, we learn so much that, by end of the visit, we are almost in a position to start our own crocodile farm when we get back home. Admittedly, getting planning permission might be a bit tricky. *Mastermind*, then, with crocodiles as our specialist subject?

Having been asked by a fellow parishioner to send him a stamped envelope from Cambodia to add to his collection, and having duly secured and addressed an envelope, we decide to return to our hotel via the post office. The problem is that we don't know the location of Battambang Post Office. Not an unusual kind of situation, one we are, in fact, quite familiar with at home, where Royal Mail, having relinquished its prime central location in the nearest town to our village, keeps moving its customer services from one improbable outlet to another. Its counters are currently nestling shyly at the back of the first floor of W.H. Smith's, where they will hopefully remain for a while. This recent aversion of Royal Mail to having branches that stay put has transformed a simple operation like sending a parcel into a kind of treasure hunt. You go to where the Post Office was last time you had occasion to use it, and there it isn't, with no indication in any shape or form of its new hiding place.

It seems that it is treasure hunt time again, Cambodian style. Not only do we not know where the post office is, but Chanthorn does not know either. The tuk-tuk driver comes to our rescue. He knows, or thinks he does. It is on the other side of town.

We alight some time later in front of a building of some architectural merit, a distant cousin of the imposing edifice back home where we used to go to to send parcels, once upon a time. It is a pleasant find, well worth having a look at. We go in and enter a cool spacious hall, with not a single queue in sight. Understandably, we find this a little disconcerting, but the staff hurry to help and could not be more amiable. We point to the address and purchase a stamp, which they assure us is of the correct value. We stick it on the envelope, put the letter in the post box, and start walking towards the door. Chanthorn is baffled: "We're leaving? Don't you have to pay for the carriage?" He has never sent a letter in his life. He has never needed to.

Who did he know besides the people of Chomnaom when he was younger? Who could read and write around him? And now, like everyone else, he has a mobile phone to communicate with. So we explain to him that stamps are not just decorative.

He is chuffed. He has had two firsts today: the crocodile farm and now this. He celebrates by taking a selfie with all of us in front of the post office. He may never have sent a letter in his life, but he is a dab hand at posting pictures on Facebook. I would not be surprised if the selfie is up before we are all settled in the tuk-tuk.

LOOKING BACK OVER 2016:
CHOMNAOM

———

Chomnaom, 2017

OM NY

None of the families we visit in Chomnaom has been affected by the kind of change experienced by our Battambang contacts. There are no new buildings to admire, just loans to repay. There are no improvements in the water supply, no major differences in the households. Life is very much like last year, rife with health problems and money concerns.

Om Ny does have an important piece of news. Her youngest daughter got married, here, in Chomnaom, a few weeks ago. She has now gone back to Sihanoukville. Om Ny comments laughingly at the irony of having such a big house, when all the children have gone. The only occupants are Om Ny herself, her husband, and a nine-year-old granddaughter.

She tells us more about the facilities. Like the installations that we saw in the city, the toilet has a septic tank, but, unlike what happens in Battambang, there are no emptying services. They get rid of the waste by using it as fertilizer. We also learn that there are no refuse collections or recycling facilities either, so it falls to them to dispose of their rubbish as best they can. What do they do with empty plastic bottles? I ask, having frequently come across piles of discarded bottles and other types of litter when touring round the countryside. They burn them, she replies.

She takes us through her daily routine. Up at 4 or 5, she starts by doing the housework. She cleans the house, does the washing, boils water for drinking. Then she has breakfast. It is her responsibility to look after the garden, so she fits this in at some point. At 12, she makes cakes that she takes to sell round the village from 1 until 3. In the afternoon, she prepares dinner, and in the evening, relaxes watching TV: the news or Thai movies. She usually goes to bed between 9 and 10 pm.

YIEY KOUM

Yiey Koum is on her own when we arrive at her house, but, once again, we are soon joined by her daughter. Yiey Koum's situation is much the same as last year. The two grandchildren who were living with her are still here, and her health remains poor. She lists the physical ailments she is plagued with (arthritis, back ache, itchy skin), but it is her persistent low spirits and her inability to ignore her complaints that come across as the main problem. She has not reconciled herself to her changed circumstances, and the lonely life she depicts is that of someone turned in on herself, trapped in depression and despondency. A state of affairs that is made worse by the enforced inactivity caused by her obvious frailty, and the ample opportunities idleness provides to dwell on your troubles.

This turns the interview into a tale of woe. As well as being concerned about her own infirmities, Yiey Koum is worried about the ill health of a son living opposite. She is upset that the son who lives in Thailand is not earning enough to be able to come back to Chomnaom for Khmer New Year. And she resents having to be supported by her children. All this seems to go round and round in her head and it is no surprise to hear that she suffers from insomnia. Unable to sleep, she gets up at 4 am. I ask what she does when she is up. "Nothing." Does she watch television? She used to, but she does not want noise, so she has stopped watching.

Before leaving, we give her a photo taken at last year's village blessing. We see a smile appear on her lips when she recognizes herself – a welcome but all too brief respite from the oppressive doom and gloom, the atmosphere of darkness and hopelessness that permeates the rest of the conversation.

OM RIM & TA JOK

Round 3 in Chomnaom is a bit of a marathon. Our daily schedule normally comprises only one interview, two at the most, but we are not spending much time in Chomnaom, so today we have three appointments.

Our next port of call is Om Rim and Ta Jok's home. As there is nothing to sit on in the room in which we are meeting, Ta Jok goes to find, or borrow, some chairs, which he hands over to us. I hesitate as I eye the fruit of his labours. Only someone who has no use for chairs would regard this as a chair. It is a relic rather than a chair, at least according to the normal meaning of the word chair as a seat with a back and four legs. True, it has a back and four legs, but the seat has all but crumbled away, developing a big hole in the middle. The overall effect is that of a toilet seat set on four legs instead of a pedestal. A one-off model designed by an eccentric afficionado of holes with ragged edges. Emboldened by my ability to squeeze into a child's seat at Om Borei's house, I risk sitting on it. Actually, there is not a lot of choice. It is the one-of-a-kind excruciatingly-uncomfortable-looking toilet seat, or the floor. Or else commandeering what

Michael has been offered, which is more recognizably a chair. I am loath to do that and the floor has not much to recommend it either. Besides, Ta Jok has lugged these "chairs" all the way up to the first floor despite his bad back, and it would be rude and churlish to spurn what he has managed to rustle up.

"I could not sleep last night", Om Rim begins, "I was worried." Different house, similar issues, except that the root of Om Rim's insomnia lies in money problems: she is worried about the repayments on their house. This too has a familiar ring. After investing 50 000 baht of savings into the rebuilding, supplemented by contributions from their children and by a $900 donation from Singapore, Om Rim and Ta Jok found themselves faced with a shortfall of 20 000 baht and turned to a local moneylender to bridge the gap.

The use of moneylenders is a widespread practice in rural Cambodia, which has a high level of poverty-induced indebtedness. Chomnoam is no exception. Over the years, we have come across several families who had recourse to moneylenders for one reason or another. Most were farmers trapped in a vicious cycle, buying seeds and fertilisers on credit from the same outfit that would buy their rice at harvest time. Other reasons for entering into loans included paying for house repairs or for hospital treatment. In one case – this time in Battambang – an elderly lady we visited had lost her house after borrowing more money than she could possibly repay within the stipulated timescale so that her sister could have a heart operation. She now lived in cramped accommodation in a corner of another sister's plot (and the sister she had borrowed for had died).

Much to our surprise we discover that there is no shortage of moneylenders in and around Chomnaom, Chinese as well as Khmer. Chinese moneylenders are reported to be better, as their rates are lower. They only charge 2%, whereas Khmer moneylenders ask for 3%. 2% seems to us most reasonable, pretty cheap, in fact. Until we get home and tot up the figures. Not entirely satisfactorily, I must confess, but convincingly enough to come to the conclusion that what our interlocutors were quoting – consistently, for their stories tallied with one another – was the interest per *month*, not per *year*.

This puts a rather different complexion on the matter and accounts for Om Rim's concerns. With a rate of 2% per annum it should not take the couple too long to pay back their loan. 25%, on the other hand, presents a serious challenge, not to mention the risk of losing their land if they do not repay what they owe. They took out a fixed term contract and a neighbour stood as guarantor. What if they managed to clear the loan earlier, I ask. They would still have to pay interest for the whole period, she replies.

Om Rim's fears may be compounded by her current inability to go out gleaning rice as she did last year. The reason she stopped is not that the landowners ceased allowing people to glean. You can still glean without special permission, it's an accepted practice. No, she did not glean because she has no energy. She still went to collect snails, though, from 6 in the morning to 6 in the evening. How many snails does she gather over a 12 hour period? "Around 12 kilos." "And how much money does this bring in?" "2000 riels per kilo." 50 US cents, 36p in GBP. For an hour's work.

It is getting more arduous as she gets older, she comments, as she can't run as fast as younger people. "Why do you have to run after snails?" Michael enquires, with some justification. She does not run after the snails. She runs because there are over 20 people following the tractor, and the first people to reach a new place get the snails near the surface. The latecomers must dig further down. It is a race and there are arguments, which she gives us a flavour of, laughing: "My snail!" "My snail!"

She is now involved in a different money making enterprise. She has switched from collecting snails to fishing. Not the leisurely activity enjoyed by anglers in countries like Britain. Or the net fishing practised on the Tonle Sap. This particular form of fishing, which we have yet to observe, involves standing waist deep in mud. The common Khmer saying *"mien tek, mien trei"* (where there is water, there is fish) is certainly true around here. Any area with water teems with fish. As the water recedes in the dry season, poor people go down into the mud to catch whatever they can. This occupation has caused Om Rim's legs to become inflamed. She is showing us the poor state of her legs when there are footsteps on the stairs. It is Yiey Koum's daughter selling crickets.

They invite her to sit down. We ask about the crickets. She explains that she buys the crickets fresh, at 5000 riels a kilo, fries them, and then goes round the village selling a can of 200 g or so of fried crickets for 2500 riels. In the same way that Om Ny goes round selling cakes.

I find this hawking of edible goods by people who have found a niche suited to the Cambodians' predilection for snacks fascinating. Throughout the day you come across villagers engaged in supporting communal nibbling, whether as providers or as consumers. Offering, between them, a kind of shared mini menu composed of dishes bought for a modest sum, a culinary village-wide game of musical chairs in which every so often cooks become purchasers. One step up from barter, part of the local culture, business on a human scale and with a human face, that doubles up as an opportunity to catch up on the latest news or gossip.

Om Rim agrees to invest in a bag of fried crickets and suggests we sample some. As it happens, we have had crickets before. One each, to be precise. They were for sale at a place we stopped at on one of our coach trips to, or from, Phnom Penh.

As we were strolling past her stall engaged in a futile search for a snack safe to eat other than crisps or biscuits, a cricket vendor encouraged us to try her produce. It was *"chngang, chngang"*, "truly delicious", she assured us, rather predictably, offering each of us a free specimen. Like most things, whether it was *chngang* was a matter of taste and debatable, unlike the fact that it was decidedly crunchy. We thanked her profusely, told a lie about it being delicious, and immediately gave ourselves away by not buying a bag of these tasty titbits.

This happened quite a while ago and we don't want to offend Om Rim, so we agree to give fried crickets a second chance. We are about to pop a couple of them in our mouths when Kounny, who is standing in for Chanthorn as our interpreter, intervenes. We can't eat the crickets as they are, he must first peel them for us and remove their legs. It is alright for Cambodians to eat unpeeled fried crickets, but we are not Cambodians, we are foreigners, and our throats are not used to eating crickets. Apparently, we could choke. With horror, I cast my mind back to the stallholder's kind gesture and our rash acceptance of her gift. Were we really unknowingly flirting with death? Who would have thought that eating a fried insect was a reckless act? Uncommon, no doubt, but life-threatening?

Later on, Om Rim takes us through her routine. Some people just lie in bed when they can't sleep. Not Om Rim. Whatever the time – occasionally 2 am, she says – she gets up, cleans the house, does the washing up. At 8 or 9, she goes down the road to have breakfast at a stall run by another villager. Michael and I splashed out a couple of years ago and tried out one of the dishes on the menu at that stall: a thin stuffed savoury pancake, a sort of Khmer equivalent of *crêpe suzette*. We both found it very *chngang*. The bill for two pancakes came to 2000 riels – less than 40p – and I am reliably informed that it is cheaper for people to go out for breakfast than try and cook their own.

Back home, Om Rim prepares lunch, eats, at 11am, and then has a rest. She does more household tasks in the afternoon. She chops wood, washes the clothes, cleans the house. If it sounds like she may be struggling with a form of Obsessive Compulsive Disorder, remember where the house is situated, the dusty roads, the absence of window panes. They have dinner between 5 and 6, after which she watches TV, mostly films, either made in Cambodia, or made in China but dubbed into Khmer. And then, at 11 pm, she goes to bed. I do not know whether she dozes in front of the television, but I would certainly find it hard to keep awake. Ta Jok does not have his wife's stamina. His day does not begin until 5.30 am and he retires at 9 pm. As time is getting on, I don't ask what he does in-between.

The conversation returns to Om Rim's ailments. She has had an echography for her knee and shows us the diagnosis, written in French, although I don't suppose this makes much difference since she does not know how to read. As well as sore

legs, she has problems with her thyroid and high blood pressure, while Ta Jok, for his part, suffers from sciatica. She explains how one of the nuns living in the church compound tours the village taking care of the health of older people, distributing medicine and providing advice.

We pass round photos of our grandchildren. They pore over them, discuss at some length what is going on in the pictures. They are surprised, on seeing a picture of one of our grandsons on a bike, that people ride bikes in our country, and marvel at the sight of an Italian ice cream. Do they have questions for us? They do. Interesting questions, signs of a friendly relationship and demonstrating an interest in life beyond Cambodia. Do we live alone? Where do our children live? And, less predictably, but not strange from their perspective, do our children send us money?

KROO YAT

All that remains to do now is to interview Kroo Yat, who has opted this year to meet with us at his house. Kroo Yat's house is behind the presbytery, which is where we are staying, so we don't have far to walk, the next day, to get there. Just a small road to cross. As we do, I notice a car parked right in front of the house. Cars are few and far between in these parts and this one is particularly big and plush. Not the sort of thing that is easy to miss, you would think. I don't know whether Michael is walking with his eyes closed at that point, but he later admits that he did not see a car.

Having heard that there are people from the United States visiting relatives living in Chomnaom, I assume that the visitors are currently calling on Kroo Yat and his family, and that the car belongs to them. It seems the sort of transport an American family would hire, and it would account for the presence of strangers chatting happily with Kroo Yat and his wife in the shaded area under the house. Plausible, but wrong. The visitors are not related to Kroo Yat or his wife. They are the money lenders, and they have come to collect some of what he owes. They lent him funds last year to buy food for the pigs he was raising. Most of the pigs have died, but the debt has to be paid off.

We have gone over to look at the pigs when the "guests" depart. Kroo Yat informs us that the harvest has been good this year, so he is happy. On the other hand, he is not happy at still owing money on dead pigs that are not going to bring him any return. Between purchasing fertilizer, weed killer, and food for the now defunct pigs, he had to borrow 40 000 baht (about $1000) and he has just handed over 15 000 baht. To crown it all, one of his daughters recently got married, and although the young couple made a contribution to the cost of the wedding, it was expensive. Like Om Rim and Ta Jok, he tells us that he prefers Chinese money lenders because their terms are better. Chinese families are rich, he remarks. You might have come to this conclusion by yourself from the look of the car parked outside when we arrived, had it happened to catch your attention.

We have heard how Om Ny and Om Rim spend their days. What about Kroo Yat? He too wakes up around 5, which is not as early as it seems if you take into account that a high percentage of the animal population are fully awake by then, not to mention the people in charge of the music announcing weddings and funerals. He gets up, has a coffee and goes to Mass, where he reads out the readings of the day. This task, or honour, depending on your point of view, would normally fall to one of the two Korean nuns who recently moved to Chomnaom, but their Khmer is not good enough yet.

Like virtually everyone else, it would appear, he then has breakfast outside, around 8.30, after which he goes to his rice field or else stays to help Fr Viney, the Cambodian priest who has taken over Fr Pedro's duties in Chomnaom. He comes back around 11 for a rest and then has lunch with his family. How many people? Currently 17, including a couple recently back from Thailand. He seems to have trouble keeping track of his family. He talked of there being around 19 people in 2015, but perhaps 17 qualifies as "around 19". Or the number keeps going up and down. Anyway, they all live with him, so it is not really surprising that he prefers to sleep downstairs, where it is quieter, rather than upstairs with the grandchildren like his wife, and that he needs a second siesta after lunch.

In the afternoon, he goes back to church, and then returns home to feed and clean the pigs. After dinner, which is at 6, he says a short prayer by himself before watching television. He watches shows, the news. He does not like the news reports. There seems to be nothing but wars and threatening developments. All he wants, personally, is for his children to love each other and to be good Catholics. He seems reasonably content, certainly happier than last year.

KOMPONG THOM

―――

March 2017

We have said goodbye to our interviewees in Chomnaom and Battambang and thanked them for opening their homes and their hearts to us. We hope to come again, yet we know that a chapter is closing. We leave with concerns, aware of our friends' increasing vulnerability and the precarious nature of their lives. Especially in Chomnaom.

Our trip is nearly over. We are flying home in a couple of days. We have arranged to spend our last two days in Cambodia in Kompong Thom, a town we have never visited. The parish priest there, Fr BongBong, is a Jesuit missionary we met before he was ordained, when he was still *Brother* BongBong, and he has invited us to come and stay with him.

Our original plan was to go to Kompong Thom at the beginning of our stay, on our way to Battambang. Or rather, since Kompong Thom is not actually on the route between Siem Reap and Battambang, but half way between Siem Reap and Phnom Penh, to begin with a short(ish) detour. However, having failed to identify a bus company selling online tickets for

Kompong Thom, we moved the trip to Kompong Thom to the end, figuring it would be easier that way.

It was – at least as far as purchasing bus tickets was concerned. We asked Fr Manoj, the new director of the Tep Im Centre. With his help, we booked both legs of the journey in Battambang. Two seats for the way there and two seats on the very first bus from Kompong Thom to Siem Reap for the day of our flight home. The Battambang office did not have a detailed schedule. They could tell us the departure time from Phnom Penh, but not the time the coach stopped to pick up passengers in Kompong Thom. Still, we would surely find that out when we got to Kompong Thom, no?

The place we have just been dropped off in Kompong Thom is not somewhere you would immediately recognise as a bus stop. It has no distinguishing features whatsoever, unless you regard the relative proximity of a restaurant serving food and drinks to weary passengers as a substitute for a non-existent bus stop sign. We had hoped to find a schedule pinned up where we alighted that would give us a clue about where and when to pick up the coach back to Siem Reap. But, of course, schedules cannot be displayed on absent signposts and although, in an ideal world, there would be a board with timetables in the restaurant nearby, the establishment does not have the slightest interest in providing this sort of information. They are there to sell food.

We later talk to Fr BongBong, who makes a series of telephone calls. The outcome of the calls is that our coach will leave Kompong Thom about half an hour after it gets there. As to when this is likely to be, well, it depends on the traffic.

We set about estimating how long the journey might take. The general opinion in the presbytery is that it is probably not too different from going by car, the mode of transport that everyone uses. How long does a car journey take? Nobody has timed this. Probably something between (*think of a number*) and (*think of another number*), according to how fast you drive, the time of day, the state of the road, not to mention where in Phnom Penh you start from.

And then there is the minor problem of where we are supposed to wait. Where we were dropped off, which is on the wrong side of the road if you are travelling from Phnom Penh to Siem Reap, or at the equivalent place on the opposite side, which would make more sense? Or perhaps somewhere else altogether. We debate the matter for a while without coming to any firm conclusion, not least because practice varies, it emerges, between different bus companies, according to the café, or cafés, that they patronize. It looks as if, in an effort to maintain a pleasing symmetry between the beginning and the end of our trip, the cloud of uncertainly that hovered over the first stage has started to descend on the last. But there is more than a day to go and no cause for alarm.

Fr BongBong has drawn up a programme for us. It is not quite what we envisaged for our last day in Cambodia, but it is something we have never done before and we like adventures. Before joining the Jesuits, Fr BongBong studied electrical engineering. Tomorrow is his free day and he plans to spend most of it sorting out the wiring of the presbytery. He does not expect us to help, which, in truth, might prove too much of an adventure for all of us. Instead, he has arranged for us to accompany one of his staff, who has to distribute six Mekong wheelchairs to people living in the countryside.

Originally designed for landmine victims, the Mekong wheelchair, which has three wheels instead of the standard four, was conceived with the rough terrain of rural Cambodia in mind. It is manufactured in Banteay Prieb, a training centre near the capital established by the NGO Jesuit Service Cambodia in 1991 for people with disabilities. It is a common sight in the prefecture, because of the number of landmine victims living there, but it is also used more widely outside by stroke victims and accident casualties.

When we meet Thim, our guide for the day, the next morning, he tells us how delighted he is that we are coming with him. Not least because it has prompted Fr BongBong to lend him his pick-up truck, thereby enabling him to deliver all the wheelchairs in one go, instead of having to make several trips on his motorbike. (The wheelchairs come in bits and are assembled in situ.)

We drive for quite a while before turning off the main road, a newly built expressway, built by the Chinese, we are told, that would make anyone living in the depths of East Anglia turn green with envy. And there, amidst the trees, not 100 metres from the busy 21st century intent on speeding to wherever it is busily speeding to, lies a totally different world. An alternative, parallel universe. The contrast is so stark that it leaves me reeling, screaming inside. It is shocking. Utterly, profoundly, shocking.

We stop outside a small modern hut reached via a short flight of ladder-like steps. We, or more accurately Thim, have not come here to deliver one of the wheelchairs that have been loaded in the back of the truck, but to repair a wheelchair that has developed a fault. "Oh, she is not at home", he exclaims, as we get out of the vehicle. "This is odd, I rang her, she knew we were coming. She must have gone out." We are standing on the edge of a wooded area and the place is deserted. He wisely decides to wait a few minutes.

"Oh, here she is; she went to pick something in the forest", we hear him exclaim a while later. I look round. There is no one in sight. I attempt to follow his gaze. All I can see is a track across the grass leading into the jungle with, in the distance, what looks like an empty self-propelled wheelchair coming in our direction. Until the wheelchair gets closer before finally stopping in front of us. And then I see her. When we are introduced, I try to look at her eyes and her lovely wavy brown hair, and to conceal my dismay at the stumps that are her legs, at the right arm ending below the elbow, the left arm dangling over the side that she uses to turn the wheels and move the chair around and that ends with a hand with only three fingers. I have forgotten her name, but she is not someone I am likely to forget.

She needs to get out of the wheelchair so that Thim can repair it. I look at the steps incredulously. How strange to build a house with steps she can't possibly get up. I must have blinked, for all of a sudden, there she is at the top of the steps. I am so taken aback that I literally blurt out: "How did she get there?", but she is coming down again and Michael won't have to explain. She walks on her stumps.

Later, Thim tells us that she was born like this and used to live with her mother, until her mother died two years ago.

Keeping up her lifelong struggle for independence, she now lives on her own. There is a well in the plot of land in front of the house from which she draws water, though how she manages is beyond me. She cooks, she keeps both the house and herself clean. She used to sell bicycle parts to raise some money, but found this difficult as people were reluctant to buy from her. So Jesuit Service Cambodia, which, if I am not mistaken, rebuilt the house, do their best to offer some support.

We talk to her a little, and then take some group photos. We have just finished when it occurs to me that all the photos were taken with us standing up. We should have been at her level. We start again. The ground is too hard to kneel on, so I am crouching by her side, a position difficult to hold for very long. I implore: "Hurry up, hurry up!" But, of course, we need *muy tiet, muy tiet* (another one, and another one). Feeling myself in danger of collapsing on the floor, I start giggling. Which is good, for I can feel tears welling up and the laughter makes it easier to hold them back. If you look at the photos of the three of us you won't see the tears, but they are there. On the inside.

The rest of the morning is spent distributing the new wheelchairs. On the way to the next houses Thim explains that 99% of the beneficiaries are Buddhist. They are mostly stroke victims and tend to be referred by community leaders. Thim visits the person, assesses the case, the size of wheelchair needed, and, where appropriate, puts the person's name on the waiting list. He also monitors how they are doing once they have the wheelchair, and comes to collect it if it is no longer needed.

The actual distribution stirs up in me a strange cocktail of discordant emotions. The people we visit have been waiting for a wheelchair for weeks, unable to leave their bed without help, including to go to the toilet. Seeing them lying on a wooden platform waiting to be given a modicum of independence brings home the frustration, the distress they must have experienced. The poverty of the surroundings, the far-reaching repercussions of becoming incapacitated, unable to work, the people's uncertain future, do nothing to lift your spirits. But their joy and that of their family when Thim joins us after assembling the longed-for wheelchair is contagious. There then follows a set of recommendations, for the individual themselves and also for their carers, as well as a driving lesson. A crucial, good-humoured event, watched by the whole family. Then it is on to the next visit.

The afternoon is quieter. Fr BongBong takes us to Kompor Kor, a beautiful, peaceful place. It was Bishop Michael's favourite and summons up memories of him. We would not be here but for the twinning that he set up. After dinner, we all repair to a service station, not for fuel, but enticed by the seductive prospect of a cold drink and a breath or two of technologically-cooled fresh air.

On the day of our departure we think it best to play it safe, and set off early to take our positions on the main road. We suspect that, if the worst comes to the worst, Fr BongBong will drive us to the airport, but we'd rather he did not have to. Instead of waiting quietly in the presbytery, we choose to spend the morning, or most of it, peering down the road from Phnom Penh, ready to seize our luggage and make a run for it. We begin by standing in front of the café near the spot where we were dropped off on the way in, move to the right, stand a little more forward, check the destination of any coach, bus, minibus, stopping nearby, in case the company is using a vehicle of a different size, or colour, from the one that brought us here. It is a good thing the receptionist of the Siem Reap hotel is not here. She would not hesitate to label us as neurotics.

Our coach eventually turns up, stopping, needless to say, on the other side of the road and near a different café. Dodging the traffic, we make a dash for it, complete with suitcases. There are two free seats, duly reserved for us, and even time to take our cue from the other passengers, who have gone in search of refreshments.

By the time we reach Siem Reap, our plane has become a kind of Holy Grail. We scrap the idea of visiting our favourite restaurant in Siem Reap and catch a tuk-tuk straight to the airport. A look at the departure board fails to enlighten us as to which check-in desk we are to report to. By now, our initial calm has given way to a slight propensity to anxiety. We are not hysterical. We just do not want to miss the plane. We ask around. The check-in desk number appears to be a well-kept secret. Or else check-in desk numbers are decided by drawing lots, and change from day to day. When the elusive information is finally displayed, we are at the wrong end of the hall. We hasten to the right place to discover that a huge queue has already assembled. More of a scrum, really, or whatever is the technical term for a group of people pushing this way and that. We while away the time by discussing the overbooking of planes and the likelihood of being bumped. You can hear the hotel receptionist tut tutting behind us. We do make it onto the plane. The couple behind us don't.

What happens next is another story.

REFERENCES

Bourboulon, M-L. (2017). *Charles Badré, Oncle Charly, Père Jean o.s.b.* Publisher: Bourboulon, ISBN 978-2-9557675-0-4.

Chigas, G. and Mosyakov, D. (n.d.). *Literacy and Education under the Khmer Rouge*, Genocide Program Studies, Yale University, accessed 10 January 2017, <https://gsp.yale.edu/literacy-and-education-under-khmer-rouge>.

Figaredo Alvargonzález, E. (2012). Interview by Lozano, M. in *A martyr church: Cambodian Catholics remember their heroes*, ZENIT.org, accessed 5 August 2019, <https://zenit.org/articles/a-martyr-church-cambodian-catholics-remember-their-heroes/>.

Ponchaud, F. (1990). *The cathedral of the rice paddy: 450 years of history of the Church in Cambodia*. (N. Pignarre, Transl.). Paris: Le Sarment – Fayard.

Rodríguez Olaizola, J. M. (2016). *The heart of the lonely tree*. (Milton Elliot Jensen, Transl.). Maliaño: Editorial Sal Terrae.

Ross, R. R. (1990). *Cambodia: a country study*, Area handbook series, Federal Research Division, Library of Congress, accessed 5 August 2019, <https://cdn.loc.gov/master/frd/frdcstdy/ca/cambodiacountrys00ross/cambodiacountrys-00ross.pdf>.

Shawcross, W. (1979). *Sideshow: Kissinger, Nixon and the destruction of Cambodia*. London: André Deutsch.

Ung, L. (2016). *First they killed my father: a daughter of Cambodia remembers*. Edinburgh: Mainstream Publishing.

ACKNOWLEDGEMENTS

———

Many people have helped with the writing of this book. First and foremost, my interviewees, who trusted me and provided me with so much material, and whose story it is. Thanks are due to all those who have assisted us over the years: Bishop Michael Evans (RIP) and Monsignor Enrique Figaredo, who, by twinning their two dioceses, triggered our interest in Cambodia and inspired us to go and see; Fr Totet Banaynal, our first host; the people who made practical arrangements for us, took us around, and made us feel welcome.

Thank you to Fr Pedro Gomez, who helped organize the interviews, for his friendship, and for supporting the project from beginning to end. Thanks too, to Chanthorn Chom and Kounny Chhoum, for their patient interpreting, for listening to and translating some difficult memories.

Thanks to Mary Fox, Pedro, and Michael, for reading my drafts and for their comments and suggestions. I am, of course, responsible for any errors that remain. Thank you to Stella Fox for permission to use her photo of the Lokta Damborng statue, and to Michael for the other pictures.

From the very start Michael has been central to the project. I thank him from the bottom of my heart for being there at my side, offering not only much needed practical help, but also reassurance and encouragement through the moments of self-doubt.

AUTHOR PROFITS FROM THE SALE OF THIS BOOK
WILL BE DONATED TO ORGANISATIONS THAT
SUPPORT THOSE IN NEED IN CAMBODIA